D0829931

FRESH INSIGHTS
TO END THE
GLASS CEILING

FRESH INSIGHTS

TO END THE

GLASS CEILING

*New Research and Solutions to Make
the Glass Ceiling a Thing of the Past*

—

NANCY E. PARSONS

LEADER VOICE PUBLISHERS
CDR ASSESSMENT GROUP, INC.

LEADER VOICE PUBLISHERS
A division of
CDR Assessment Group, Inc.
Sugar Land, TX

cdrinfo@cdrassessmentgroup.com

Copyright © Nancy E. Parsons, 2017

All rights reserved. No part of this book may be reproduced, stored in, or introduced into a retrieval system, or transmitted in any form, or by any means (electronic, mechanical, photocopying, recording, or otherwise) without the prior written permission of the copyright owner Nancy E. Parsons.

Printed in The United States of America by CreateSpace, an Amazon company. Also distributed electronically by Kindle, an Amazon Company.

ISBN 978-0692855744

www.cdrassessmentgroup.com
Twitter: @CDR_Assessment   @NEParsons

This book can be purchased in print and via Kindle at www.amazon.com

Book design by K. M. Weber, www.ilibribookdesign.com

DEDICATION

This is for Mary Frizzell, who was my executive assistant back in the 1980s. She was assigned to me in my role as director of human resources after she had worked for the vice president of operations for many years. Mary was in her 50s at the time. She never had the chance to advance because she was *a woman and a mother*. She was brilliant in so many ways and respected by all; so were Patty, Ferle, the other Mary, my mother Nancy, and many more women back in those days.

Contents

Acknowledgments

There are many people who have contributed to this effort whom I would like to sincerely thank. First is my business partner, Kimberly Leveridge, Ph.D., who joined me in 1998 and took the chance to launch our firm, CDR Assessment Group, Inc., and develop our assessments, which remain unmatched to this day. Kim continues to serve as our Scientific Advisor.

Thanks also to Lynn Flinn, Annette White-Klososky, Donna Miller, and Tanis Cornell, facilitators and licensed operators of EWF International forums in Tulsa, Oklahoma City, and Dallas, for inviting me to work with their corporate executive women and CEO groups to help us collect more data and present our findings along the way. Thanks as well to the talented women in those executive groups! I enjoyed all the meetings, feedback, and offsite sessions. Thank you to my colleague, Patricia Wheeler, Ph.D., for contributing the article "Worry Less, Lead Better" which can be found in the Appendix. I would also like to express gratitude to my Alexcel Group colleagues who are inspiring and supportive always.

Thanks to Christine Klatt, Ana Jacome, Ed White, and the CDR Team—you rock! I appreciate your support, efforts, edits, sense of humor, and hard work. You are all a joy to work with and I am thankful you chose to work for CDR (and me). A special thanks to Bonnie Budzowski for her editorial support and guidance.

Last and not least in any way, I thank my husband, Bill. While he has a very demanding career as a chief medical officer, he's always supported my work and my sometimes over-the-top ambition. I am so blessed and thankful to have Bill in my life.

Preface

At CDR Assessment Group, Inc., our goal has been to revolutionize leadership—and we are on that journey. Helping women to bring down the glass ceiling is clearly part of the road to revolutionizing leadership.

- The glass ceiling exists and is still strong in 2017, with women comprising only 5.8 percent of all *Fortune* 500 CEOs;[1]
- continues to stymie millions of women's upward leadership success;
- has been misunderstood, and at last our new research has identified the root cause of why it exists and has held so steadfast;
- costs organizations billions of dollars a year in lost opportunities and performance.

Now that we have identified the true cause of this blockade, we can bring it down—swiftly!

This book is for everyone who is a woman, or who knows one. It really is that important.

Introduction

1979

Nineteen seventy-nine was a really good year for women.

That was the year I started my human resources professional career, I turned 21, and, most important, the US Pregnancy Discrimination Act went into effect.[2] This meant that women could no longer be fired for getting pregnant. Yes, back then, getting pregnant was an offense that could result in getting fired. Also, women could no longer be deemed "not promotable" because they were within their childbearing years. This meant that women, prior to the Pregnancy Discrimination Act, were legally denied promotional opportunities and were intentionally left off of succession plans for as long as twenty years, despite their performance and capabilities.

With the Pregnancy Discrimination Act and the earlier Civil Rights Act of 1964, the doors were *finally* wide open for women to be promoted based on their talent and performance. *Or so we thought.*

When I entered leadership, it was a rather new frontier for women, and I faced some interesting challenges. It didn't help that I worked at a shipyard, at a coal mine, and at petroleum pipelines, which were completely male dominated back then. Occasionally, I was blackballed or simply ignored by some of the men stakeholders I needed to deal with at those companies. Once, I received an invitation to our company's offsite HR directors meeting—two weeks after it was held (I was the only female HR director at the time).

When it came to HR back then, women were always facing uphill battles; women like Edith, who was working for a pipeline competitor and interviewing for a position at our company. Edith was a candidate for a terminal manager position. She had a mechanical engineering degree and an MBA from the University of Tulsa. Plus, Edith had been working as a petroleum product terminal supervisor for a few years. She was a great fit for the job; however, she was slightly reserved during the interview. Edith did fine but she did not oversell or come across boldly, like many of the male candidates did.

We used panel interviews for employee selection in the 1980s, and I was the only woman manager on the interview panel. During our discussion about Edith's qualifications for the position, a couple of the men said, "Well, she seems fairly capable, but she just doesn't have experience with us." *(What?! Of course she didn't! She worked for another company—our competitor.)* The other panel members were more comfortable with the less-qualified male candidates. I fought hard, and in the end, Edith was hired. She accomplished much during her tenure, which outlasted mine. Today, Edith is the health, safety, and environmental director for a top energy company.

Women Before My Time

I joined the leadership ranks at a momentous time for women because the doors were open at last. Women who were thirty, twenty, or even just ten years ahead of me rarely made it into leadership posts. Most of them dead-ended as executive or administrative assistants or as low-level professionals. Not surprisingly, there were some secretaries who were smarter and had better leadership skills than their executive bosses. The reality was that these women often ran the departments for their bosses. That was a perk their bosses enjoyed because it allowed them to spend more time on the golf course. This is not to deny that these men executives had benefitted from education that had advanced their careers, but these women were exceptional performers stuck in low-level jobs due to their gender and the social expectations of the day.

There are many stories from my earlier days—and even a couple that might shock you—but that was *then*. Fortunately, my war stories are from decades ago, and I didn't allow those antics to stop me. The good news is that things have changed considerably for the better since then, in terms of *overt* negative treatment of women. Yet there is still much work to do.

Women's Progress

In 1987, thirty years ago, the book *Breaking the Glass Ceiling* suggested,

> Many women have paid their dues, even a premium, for a chance at a top position, only to find a glass ceiling between them and their goal. The glass ceiling is not simply a barrier for an individual, based on the person's inability to handle a higher-level job. Rather, the glass ceiling applies to women as a group who are kept from advancing higher *because they are women.* [3]

So here we are today. I never imagined that, nearly *four decades* after the Pregnancy Discrimination Act passed, the following would be true:

- only 29 women, or 5.8 percent of the total number, are CEOs of *Fortune* 500 companies [4]
- "Only 14.2 % of the top five leadership positions at the companies in the S&P 500 are held by women, according to a CNNMoney analysis." [5]

And while women own 11.3 million businesses (38 percent of all businesses) in the US, [6] they are awarded less than 5 percent of government contracts. [7] Yet today more than 50 percent of college graduates are women.

The truth is, unfortunately, that the majority of women are not even in the game, let alone on the same field of play as their male counterparts. Further, many of our assumptions and beliefs about the glass ceiling are wrong. Our misperceptions have resulted in designing solutions that are just not delivering the needed results.

In Illustration 1, you can visualize how much work is still needed.

ILLUSTRATION 1
Women Under the Glass Ceiling

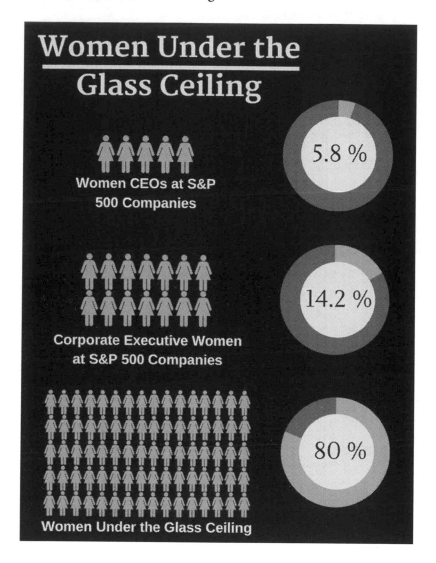

The 400-Year Wait

If we don't change the current trajectory, it will take another 400 years for women to attain 50 percent of the CEO positions. This is simply unacceptable. Let me repeat that.

Nearly four decades have passed since the Pregnancy Discrimination Act, and the glass ceiling continues to hold in place. You might wonder why I care so much, since I am at the latter stages of my career and have succeeded as an entrepreneur and business owner. My passion is

> *If we don't change the current trajectory, it will take another 400 years for women to attain 50 percent of the CEO positions.*

leadership effectiveness and development. Frankly, we have a long way to go on that journey and there is still much to do.

Also, this topic remains quite personal for me. I have two daughters with management careers, a daughter-in-law who is a surgeon, and a three-year-old granddaughter. Patience is no longer virtuous for any of us when it comes to the glass ceiling. It needs to end.

This book will answer these elusive questions:

- Are there real gender differences in leadership traits?
- What are the *real* root causes of the glass ceiling?
- How have some women made it to the top?
- Who owns the problem?
- What are the solutions? What actions should organizations and women take to end the glass ceiling phenomena?

A Quiz

Before we explain what is holding the glass ceiling in place and what we found in our research, test your current knowledge on what is causing the glass ceiling to keep such a solid footing to this day. The simple true/false quiz on the next page will test your assumptions to see how they compare to what we have learned as we have investigated deeply into this perplexing problem.

PRE-QUIZ

Test Your Knowledge About the Glass Ceiling

This is a **key** reason(s) why the glass ceiling continues to remain in place. **Mark True or False:**

TRUE OR FALSE	KEY REASON(S) FOR THE GLASS CEILING
	discrimination
	the fact that women just aren't as ambitious or driven
	promotional decision-makers favor behaviors more typically demonstrated by male leaders
	lack of sufficient government regulations and enforcement
	men are better at fighting for visibility and pushing their views
	women are judged or evaluated more harshly than men
	men are more confident in leader roles when things are tough
	women lack courage
	men tend to be less emotional than women
	women are not competitive enough
	men in leadership generally perform better than women in leadership
	women with leadership potential often need different training or development options than men

Quiz answers can be found before Chapter 6 – Solutions

ONE

The Truth About Women in Leadership and the Glass Ceiling

The Landscape of Women in Leadership Posts

During my thirty years in leadership, the glass ceiling has been a nearly impenetrable blockade, limiting the vast majority of aspiring women leaders hoping to reach the top. I am delighted to report that this book shares new research that explains why so many women have been stopped. Now we can implement needed solutions to end the glass ceiling for good.

Contrary to today's thinking and to what many studies on women in leadership suggest, we found in part one of our research, shared in Chapter 3, *that many women are actually pulling themselves out of the running based on their inherent personality-based risk factors.* We found that women who are stuck beneath the glass ceiling often have risks that differ from their male counterparts.

In the second part of our research, presented in Chapter 5, we found that the women who do make it to the top as corporate executives and as CEOs have different risk factors than the women in the original study group who were held back. These successful executive women's risks look more like the men's risks.

Can Women Lead as Effectively as Men?

Studies compiled by of the American Psychological Association repeatedly show that "one's sex has little or no bearing on personality, cognition and leadership."[8] This means that women are equally qualified, based on their inherent (measurable) capabilities, to perform as well as men in leadership.

Performance of Women in Leadership

When reviewing performance, many may find this data astonishing: women leaders are frequently rated higher on multi-rater 360° feedback than their male counterparts. In fact, Jack Zenger and Joseph Folkman reported in their 2011 survey of 7,280 leaders that "at all levels, women are rated higher in fully 12 of the 16 competencies that go into outstanding leadership."[9] In addition, a study in the *International Journal of Business Governance and Ethics* was released in 2013 stating,

Having women on the board is no longer just the right thing to do based on gender equality arguments but also the smart thing to do. Nominating committees, therefore, which ignore this fact may actually be shortchanging their investors' potential for future returns. [10]

A study of 4,000 public companies from across the globe, published by MSCI Research in 2015, found that "companies that had strong female leadership generated a Return on Equity of 10.1% per year versus 7.4% for those without." [11]

A hard-hitting report released in 2016 by Peterson Institute for International Economics was based on a peer review study of 21,980 companies from 91 countries where it was reported that: Companies with at least 30% female leaders—in senior management positions—experienced a **15 percent increase in profitability**. [12] *(Note: these results are based on a typical company with an average 6.4% net margin.)*

The Myths and the Blame Game

While the glass ceiling is real, and consequences for women and business profitability are substantial, the root causes have been elusive or misunderstood. As a result, advice frequently given to aspiring women leaders fails to help them break through barriers.

For example, Jack Welch, the former General Electric chairman and CEO, annoyed a group of women executives a couple of years ago at a forum that was sponsored by the *Wall Street Journal*. He said that the only thing that could help women's advancement to senior executive positions is to "Over deliver . . . Performance is it!" [13] The female members of the audience balked, accusing him of understanding nothing about cultural biases and how they shape the perception of performance.

Results and performance seldom tell the whole picture of successful females. While it is obvious that exceptional performance is essential, there are still too many barriers preventing women from aspiring to the C-Suite. Most would agree that Jack Welch has earned enough stripes as a leader to pontificate and speak anecdotally; however, we have empirical data that proves he is wrong on this matter. Our data shows that women actually do dig in and work hard, and when the pressure is on, many push themselves even harder than their male counterparts. Yet these same women are repeatedly bypassed for the best and most coveted positions.

Additionally, in a 2015 Pew research study of 1,835 adult respondents stated, "about four-in-ten Americans point to a double standard for women seeking to climb to the highest levels of either politics or business, where they have to do more than their male counterparts to prove themselves." [14]

Others suggest that aspiring women leaders need to

- find a worthy mentor;
- go to leadership training;
- build a network;
- assert themselves—learn to negotiate;
- get an MBA; and more. [15]

These are all worthwhile and practical developmental endeavors. Unfortunately, none of these are the *solution* to breaking the glass ceiling.

Discrimination

Some ardent feminists would have aspiring women believe that the existence of the glass ceiling is predominately due to various forms of overt discrimination such as job segregation (keep those women out!), the good-old-boy network, gender discrimination, sexual harassment; and the lack of enforcement of anti-discrimination laws. [16]

While there are pockets of discrimination that need to be addressed in timely and effective ways, discrimination is not the primary reason the glass ceiling stays strong. Furthermore, the "victim" mentality is not productive, and it sets up ambitious women to be defensive and cynical, all of which are counterproductive to the positive inroads they need to make.

Men's Views on the Glass Ceiling

We can't ignore the perceptions of men—in particular, those of most male executives, who don't recognize the glass ceiling or see the true magnitude of the problem. It's just not personal for them. Clearly, they are not tuned in to how the glass ceiling impacts the bottom line.

Most male executives go through the motions of sponsoring

and supporting "diversity councils" and "women-in-leadership initiatives" at a distance, but these actions are not producing the change and sustainable impact needed to end the glass ceiling. "Diversity" and "women in leadership" are convenient topics to pass off to others. In this way, male C-Suite members check the box that they are doing something about it, allowing them to focus on more important or "real" business issues. Whenever I present at leadership conferences on the topic "Cracking the Code to the Glass Ceiling," male leaders seldom attend. Women fill the rooms. This demonstrates that the glass ceiling is simply not a topic of keen interest or a serious matter for most men. They usually only attend when they are *required* to for mandated diversity and sexual harassment training.

Tokenism is also still in play. Too often, we see women promoted to executive positions who aren't nearly as qualified for the role as many other women. However, men executives sometimes select what we refer to as "pleasers" and other obedient or reserved female administrators who will execute as needed. These token executive women don't cause trouble. And, again, they check off the affirmative action box. While this does not represent most of the women in executive positions today, there are still too many women who are promoted due to their gender and agreeableness versus their capability, creativity, boldness, and strategic spiritedness. Tokenism hurts progress for women and fosters the self-fulfilling false prophecy about the lackluster capability of women in leadership.

Apathy about the glass ceiling isn't a mindset for only the mature men well into their leadership careers. According to a Harvard University poll of young Americans reported in 2016,

> When 18- to 29-year-olds were asked whether a glass ceiling
> (a barrier to advancement in a profession) exists for women in
> America today, nearly three in five (59%) indicated yes. Young
> women are significantly more likely to believe a glass ceiling
> exists (68%), compared to men (50%). [17]

Young men are less inclined than young women to believe that women still face the glass ceiling. But men are not the ones directly hurt by, and not the ones who have their careers stymied by, the glass ceiling. It's not personal for them. Therefore, they tend to not notice.

A cynical view would be that as we correct this obstacle for women, men in turn would achieve *fewer* of the coveted positions.

An optimistic view would say, there is plenty of opportunity for all who achieve and perform well as leaders because business opportunities will expand. (I prefer the latter point of view, *or the "blue ocean" way of thinking.*)

Implications of the 2016 Presidential Election Results

While this book is not about politics, I would be remiss if I didn't mention the implications of the historical 2016 presidential election cycle. The glass ceiling has been given prime-time attention with former Secretary of State Hillary Clinton's presidential run and with the Women's March the day after the 2017 Presidential Inauguration. Many believe that the glass ceiling phenomena was a key factor in Secretary Clinton's loss to Donald Trump. There is also an argument to be made that Clinton had long before, as secretary of state and as a US senator from New York, broken through the glass ceiling by achieving those top posts.

With this election, however, Trump was a very unlikely winner, as his loss was incorrectly predicted by all polls leading up to the 2016 election. After Clinton's actual loss, one European headline read,

2016: THE YEAR WOMEN BANGED THEIR HEADS AGAINST THE GLASS CEILING.

A lot of us expected the first female president of the United States to be elected this week. She wasn't. [18]

Did the glass ceiling contribute to Clinton's loss? Absolutely. However, I believe that her loss was affected far less by the glass ceiling than by other factors. The low turnout by her supporters in essential states, the lack of a clear and compelling campaign brand, and the rebuke by voters of President Obama's policies (i.e. Obamacare, immigration, etc.) were key factors in her loss. Of course, other issues, policy disagreements, and external forces affected the election results as well.

This is not to say that gender bias didn't play a role. However, those voters held back by misogynistic views were likely not part of Clinton's voting base to begin with.

Many believe Secretary Clinton might have won had she run a better campaign all the way through. The media's consistently erroneous polls distorted her team's confidence. This unwarranted confidence, in turn, caused their efforts to wane in the last days of the campaign because they thought they couldn't lose. Millions of people, particularly women, were crushed that the first woman presidential candidate from a major political party lost the election.

However, there is an important and positive result to be considered. It is wonderful news that a woman was the 2016 presidential candidate for a major political party in the United States. That historical distinction makes Secretary Clinton a role model for aspiring women in politics of all parties. We should honor and applaud that accomplishment, no matter our political views.

TWO

The Research

About CDR Assessment Group, Inc. and the Assessments Used in the Study

When we formed CDR in 1998, our vision was to revolutionize leadership. Helping women to break through the glass ceiling has clearly been part of this journey.

My business partner, Kimberly Leveridge, Ph.D., and I developed the CDR Character Assessment and CDR Risk Assessment in 1998 and early the next year released the CDR Drivers & Reward Assessment, completing the CDR 3-Dimensional Assessment Suite®. To this day, these assessments are considered to be unmatched coaching tools by many due to the level of details and nuanced characteristics revealed, and have been used in every sector by thousands of leaders around the globe.

The CDR 3-D Suite is primarily used for executive coaching and for leadership and team development. However, many of our clients also use these tools for selection and succession planning, since the tools are scientifically validated for these purposes as well.

For the research in this book, we focused primarily on the study results using the CDR Risk Assessment, which identifies risks that can lead to derailment. Secondarily, we used the CDR Character Assessment, which measures the inherent strengths, or bright sides of personality, of the respective groups.

Our Original Study Was *Not* About the Glass Ceiling

We were originally conducting research comparing 360° Leader Scan multi-rater feedback results to the CDR Risk Assessment* results but then expanded our review because we noticed significant (and unexpected) gender differences. This propelled us to begin looking more closely at the gender-based differences that we inadvertently discovered when reviewing the CDR Risk Assessment results of the men and women study groups, and it became our first study on the glass ceiling.

---

*See study results presented at International Society of Performance Improvement International, Vancouver, 2006 – CDR White Paper: "Comparing Leadership Risk Factor Results to 360° Feedback." [19]

Research Overview:

- Comparing inherent personality risk assessment results of mid-level men and women leader study groups (part one of the study)
- Analyzing CDR Character and Risk Assessment results compared to Pew Cultural Survey results about the perceptions of men and women leaders (part one of the study compared to Pew research data)
- Comparing the first CDR study groups' personality data (character and risks) to corporate executive women and CEO/entrepreneurial women groups (part two of the study)

The Study Participants

In the first part of the study, which is discussed in Chapter 3, we reviewed the CDR Risk Assessment results of mid-level leaders: 137 women and 122 men from 35 companies. In the second part of our study, reported in Chapter 5, we analyzed the personality assessment results of 30 corporate executive women and 21 women CEO/entrepreneurs who were members in Executive Women's Forum (EWF) International groups. Leaders in each of our studies were from more than 80 companies.

CDR Personality Assessments Used in the Research

Personality assessment is useful for describing an individual's characteristics that might not be directly observed. Behaviors are visible to people, but the reasons behind them and the motivations for them are not observable. Psychological assessment results provide a vocabulary for describing propensities and a view of the "whys" behind the behaviors. This information in turn allows for more effective employee selection, succession planning, team building, and professional development. In the study results shared in Chapter 3 and Chapter 5, two personality-based assessments were used: 1) CDR Risk Assessment; and 2) CDR Character Assessment. The primary emphasis of our research results is based on the CDR Risk Assessment results.

CDR Character Assessment

This personality instrument identifies individual distinctions and measures leader acumen, vocational suitability or "best fit" roles, emotional intelligence, key strengths, and potential gaps or short sides. This assessment describes the compelling and impactful performance and behavior implications of an individual's character attributes from a business and leadership development perspective. This assessment is scientifically validated for employee selection and succession planning purposes, although CDR primarily uses this data for leadership development coaching and other related services.

Table 1 shows the CDR Character Assessment scales and what each character trait measures.

TABLE 1

CDR Character Assessment Scale Titles and Descriptions

CHARACTER SCALE* TITLE	DESCRIPTION OF THE CHARACTER TRAIT
Adjustment	calm, self-assured, and steady under pressure versus self-critical, edgy, and an intense performer.
Leadership Energy	inclined to take charge, be leader-like and decisive, be interested in upward career mobility, and be highly competitive versus having tendencies to avoid leadership roles, prefer not to direct others, and are not concerned with upward mobility as a measure for success.
Sociability	is outgoing, enjoys social interaction, is extroverted, and is stimulated by dialoging with others versus having more introversion tendencies such as preferring less social interaction, maintaining a lower profile, keeping to oneself, and being quiet and perhaps shy.
Interpersonal Sensitivity	warm, caring, sensitive toward the needs of others, interpersonally skilled and perceptive versus task focused, hard-nosed, and apathetic toward the needs of others.
Prudence	practical, conscientious, self-controlled and disciplined, steady, reliable, stable, and logical in a steadfast way versus spontaneous, a risk taker, adventurous, potentially creative, adaptable, and inventive.
Inquisitive	adventurous, clever, original, creative, imaginative, and curious versus practical, task and process focused, detail oriented, and more down to earth.
Learning Approach	typically seeking learning for the sake of personal enrichment and has academic interests versus being more interested in practical educational approaches such as on-the-job training and hands-on learning.

SOURCE: Nancy Parsons and Kimberly Leveridge, Ph.D., *CDR Character Assessment* (CDR Assessment Group, Inc., 1998).

*Regarding the above character assessment scales, each of these scales has many "subscales" in the actual report that provide for more robust individual differentiation during the coaching and development process.

CDR Risk Assessment

This personality measure identifies eleven inherent risk factors and related behaviors that can erode performance and lead to derailment. Gone unchecked, these risks can drive even the most promising careers off track. It is important to recognize one's own risks in order to develop, neutralize or manage them more productively.

Table 2 shows the CDR Risk Assessment scale and what each risk factor measures.

TABLE 2
CDR Assessment Risk Factors

RISK FACTOR SCALE TITLE	DESCRIPTION OF THE RISK FACTOR
False Advocate	has passive-aggressive tendencies; appears outwardly supportive while covertly resisting
Worrier	demonstrates unwillingness to make decisions due to fear of failure or criticism
Cynic	is skeptical, mistrustful, pessimistic, and always looking for problems; constantly questions decisions; resists innovation
Rule Breaker	ignores rules, tests the limits, does what feels good, risks company resources, does not think through consequences
Perfectionist	micro-manages, clings to details, has a high need to control, has compulsive tendencies, sets unreasonably high standards
Egotist	is self-centered, has a sense of entitlement and superiority, takes credit for others' accomplishments, is a hard-nosed competitor

Table 2 continues on the next page.

TABLE 2 (CONTINUED)
CDR Assessment Risk Factors

RISK FACTOR SCALE TITLE	DESCRIPTION OF THE RISK FACTOR
Pleaser	depends on others for feedback and approval, is eager to please the boss, avoids making decisions alone, won't challenge status quo, refuses to rock the boat
Hyper-Moody	has unpredictable emotional swings, moodiness, volatility, potentially explosive outbursts, and vacillation of focus
Detached	withdraws, fades away, fails to communicate, avoids confrontation, is aloof, tunes others out
Upstager	is excessively dramatic and histrionic, dominates meetings and airtime, is constantly selling a personal vision and viewpoint, demonstrates inability to go with the tide
Eccentric	quite unusual in their thinking and behaving, perhaps whimsical, weird, out of social step or norms, peculiar in some ways

SOURCE: Nancy Parsons and Kimberly Leveridge, Ph.D., *CDR Character Assessment* (CDR Assessment Group, Inc., 1998).

Pew Cultural Survey

The Pew Cultural Survey Report referenced in this book is a summary of key trends, over time, in the movement of women into leadership positions in politics, business, and other labor force professions. In Chapter 5, we introduce the cultural bias of men versus women and then compare these Pew survey results to CDR Personality results.

The Pew survey obtained results from telephone interviews with a nationally representative sample of 2,250 adults living in the continental United States.

More Information

More details about the research methodology, assessments, validity, and the Pew survey can be found in Appendix I.

THREE

The Root Causes of Why the Glass Ceiling Exists

Essentially, there are *two* key reasons why the glass ceiling exists. One, not surprisingly, has to do with perceptions and biases. We will share research in the next chapter on why this perception issue is far more damaging and pervasive than most think. First, however, we will reveal our exciting new research findings that provide a much clearer path to *implementable* solutions.

We've spent nearly two decades measuring the personality and motivational traits of leaders and executives. Interestingly, the overall leadership characteristics or inherent personality strengths as measured by our CDR Character Assessment between male and women leaders are remarkably similar, which means that both sexes are quite capable of leader posts at the highest levels. This supports the previously-mentioned APA studies set forth in their publication, "Men and Women: No Big Difference." [20]

The "Break-through" Finding

Our "break-through" (pun intended) to ending the glass ceiling came as a result of the CDR Risk Assessment. [21] This instrument measures inherent personality risk factors, or ineffective coping strategies, that undermine performance and can derail success. These risks tend to show under stress, conflict, and pressure. Think of how often high stress and adversity is present in organizations or in leadership jobs today. I think it is safe to say that the pressure is fairly constant.

Women Are "Worriers"

Ironically, when facing adversity and pressure, women do what Jack Welch suggested—they dig in, work harder, outperform, analyze, research, often become sleep deprived, and work harder again. The CDR Risk Assessment study results from 35 companies revealed that women leaders tended to be more predominately "Worriers."

What is the CDR Risk Assessment?

This instrument measures eleven specific risk factors that can potentially end, limit, or have substantial negative impact on leadership success. Another way to think about this information is to consider these risk factors as the "dark sides" of personality. These dark sides reveal themselves over time (i.e., once the honeymoon is over) and are especially evident under times of stress.

This assessment is based upon a scientifically validated psychological assessment tool that measures the occupational and organizational risk factors of normal personality. The normative data of the CDR Risk Assessment Report are generated entirely from the results of working adults, not students or clinical patients.

Excerpted from CDR Risk Assessment report introduction.

WORRIER ▪ This scale represents an unwillingness to make decisions due to fear of failure or criticism. "Worriers" impede progress, over-study, over-review, and slow down performance. Worriers are not decisive, seem to lack courage, and fail to adapt promptly to changing demands.

Examples: Stonewalling decisions; having associates perform unnecessary non-value-added tasks just to appease personal comfort level; and being slow to act and risk aversive. [22]

Men Are "Egotists," "Rule Breakers" and "Upstagers"

So, while many women leaders scored high as Worriers, their male counterparts showed a statistically significant difference in their CDR Risk Assessment results. Men leaders tended to be "Egotists," "Rule Breakers," and "Upstagers" under adversity and conflict.

The Crux of the Problem

The missing part of understanding why the glass ceiling exists up to this point has been the unrecognized reality that women leaders go into Worrier or fear-of-failure mode. They study, analyze and re-study when working under conflict or adversity. Their fearful, cautious, and *moving-away-from-conflict* approach results in women being judged as lacking courage and confidence. There are unwritten expectations that leaders do not, and should not, run away or back down from tough issues or conflict.

> *The missing part of understanding why the glass ceiling exists up to this point has been the unrecognized reality that women leaders go in to Worrier or fear-of-failure mode.*

Men's Risks Are Viewed as More "Leader-like"

The essential point is that the men, in greater numbers, are "Moving Against," fighting for resources and airtime, and aggressively winning the day, albeit with over-the-top pushy, in-your-face, and "brave" tendencies. Men win the perception battle as they stay in the game with stamina to fight to the end while women run away, study, and analyze some more. Under pressure, more women tend to be cautious decision-makers and to slow up the process. Men push forward with speed and force. Clearly, these overconfident and aggressive behaviors, which are exhibited more by men leaders, are viewed as "leader-like" by the promotional power brokers.

Women Pulling Themselves Out of the Running

The existence of the glass ceiling is evidence that it has not been going well for the women. Essentially and to their detriment, when under pressure, many women default to ineffective coping strategies; self-defeating, diminishing behaviors that take them out of the leadership limelight and pipeline, promotionally speaking.

Women need to help women *stop* resorting to these natural self-defeating and self-doubting tendencies and to learn ways to manage, neutralize and prevent the Worrier behaviors from derailing their visibility, upward mobility, and success. One way to facilitate development is with individual assessment and coaching to help women (and men) understand and manage their own risks, particularly the Worrier tendency, more productively. For example, to especially target that tendency, our firm hosts a webinar titled "Don't Worry—Be Decisive!" and all attendees thus far have been women leaders.

Sheryl Sandberg is a successful executive from Facebook who is a self-described classic Worrier. She wrote the popular book *Lean In: Women, Work, and the Will to Lead.* In *Lean In,* Sandberg shares how she has learned to conquer, or at least quell, her fears and self-doubt:

> I also know that in order to continue to grow and challenge
> myself, I have to believe in my own abilities. I still face situations
> that I fear are beyond my capabilities. I still have days when I
> feel like a fraud. And I still sometimes find myself spoken over
> and discounted while men sitting next to me are not. But now
> I know how to take a deep breath and keep my hand up. I have
> learned to sit at the table. [23]

Ms. Sandberg is keenly self-aware and has developed ways to manage and neutralize her tendencies toward worrying and fearfulness. Aspiring women leaders who have this Worrier trait can do the same. While training and development or wishing cannot erase this risk factor, carefully thought out and practiced developmental tactics can go a long way in managing, neutralizing or preventing the risks so that they do not take women away from the table.

In addition, executives need to understand the ways many women tend to cope—and to be partners in helping those women learn more productive ways to deal with conflict and stress. Executives need to refrain from being overly jaded about a woman's tendency to worry, because this frequently results in a fatalistic or stalled career trajectory for her. We saw in the studies cited in Chapter 1 that women often outperform when in leader roles. Women have amazing talent, knowledge, and skills as leaders—and in all career vocations—so it is time we begin to appreciate their capability, while understanding that all leaders and people have risk factors.

Illustration 2 shows the averaged CDR Risk Assessment results of our study of a random selection of men and women leaders across 35 organizations. In examining the data, women have statistically significant, more than 5 percentage points, higher Worrier scores and men have statistically significant higher scores in "Egotist," "Rule Breaker" and "Upstager."

ILLUSTRATION 2
CDR Risk Assessment Average Scores ▪ Original Study Group

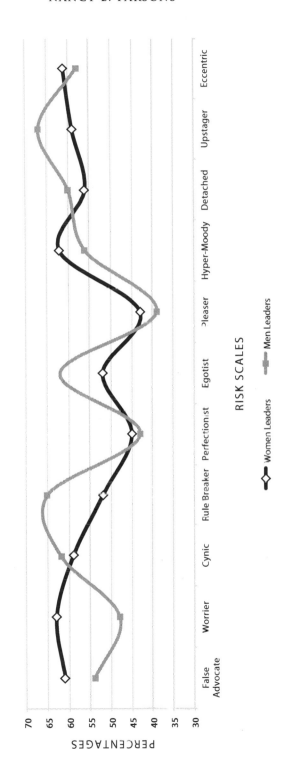

Why Are Risks So Important?

Risks are part of one's hard wiring, like it or not. These are not aspects of our personality that we can just wish away, nor can we pretend that they don't exist. They do show, or manifest, when we feel uncomfortable and stressed, and when we are faced with pressure or conflict. Here's the big problem with risks: because they have become ingrained behaviors over our lifetime, or natural responses to certain stimuli, we seldom realize we are doing these things. We may recognize that we are not at our best, but frequently we don't realize how we are undermining our own effectiveness. So, when our risks are left to run unchecked, we can be hurting ourselves, or our teams and clients, without even realizing or intending to do so.

The most important aspect of dealing with risk factors is identifying them. Once we know what our risk tendencies are, we can then begin to

- **understand what triggers them**—who (person, role, authority) and what circumstances cause them to present (when I am confronted without fair warning, when my peer pushes my buttons, when people aren't prepared . . .)
- **think of when they show** most often (when I am tired, angry, tense, etc.)
- **identify what the impact** has been on self and others
  - did I offend someone?
  - was I ignored?
  - was my aggression off-putting or alienating?
  - did I turn people off?
  - did I suffer in silence?
  - did I lose an opportunity to shine? etc.
- *most important*—**explore what one can do** to prevent, neutralize, or manage these specific risks more effectively.

Women Leaders Who Are "Worriers" Share Their Struggles

Below, several women leaders and colleagues share the challenges they routinely face as Worriers and the impact of their behaviors on their effectiveness, work-life balance, and success.

ANN

*CEO of Creative Services/Communications
and Marketing Firm*

One time I was brought into a complicated business issue with one of my business divisions. Thinking the worst, I brought the whole team down with my negative speculation and over-thinking. The team could sense my fear and they all began to fear the situation as well. It turned out to be a simple solution with the client, and I felt like a fool. I saw that my fear harmed my team. My fear even caused one valuable team member to feel inadequate and concerned for her future with our company.

There are times I wake up at night and try to process business challenges, overthinking and overanalyzing to the point to where I cannot go back to sleep. Over and over . . . every night. I think it takes me longer to make decisions because of this fear-based operation in my head.

On the flip side, the Worrier in me has kept me from making some bad decisions and always keeps me on my toes. I am acutely aware of threats and challenges and I certainly know how to dodge bullets. In some strange way, using my fear more productively has made me a stronger leader and has allowed me to grow a successful, sustainable business.

As a Worrier who leads people, I worry most about these three things: money, people, and business excellence. My business must have the right people working for the right people, make money, and do a good job every day. When any of these three is in jeopardy, I worry. ∎

MELANIE

Executive Vice President, Energy Company

Even as an executive vice president, there were times I should have given my opinion; I knew I was right, but I worried about how my opinion would be perceived if I did not have the time to prepare both my approach and tone. As a result, I missed the opportunity to demonstrate my leadership and competence and to openly contribute to important conversations of the senior leadership team. ▪

DIANE

*President, Women's Entrepreneurial
Leadership Organization*

I went back to complete my MBA more than ten years after I got my bachelor's degree. I was a married adult student with a full-time job.

In one of my very first assignments after returning to school, we were asked to write a paper on a key business issue. I spent forty hours preparing this paper over the following week. I worked until late at night (after getting off work) and over the weekend to get it done in time. I was worried about what the teacher expected of me and didn't want to fail.

After we turned in our papers, the teacher indicated that he had just expected us to spend a couple hours completing the assignment.

As a working person, I had gone into hyperdrive because I was worried about getting a good grade on one paper (something that, in reality, would have had a minimal impact on my life or career, even if had been mediocre).

I have since gotten much better about determining expectations before embarking on a new project. ▪

KATHY

*Business Manager of consulting firm and recent director of largest
division of manufacturer of industrial materials*

As a Worrier, I had a tendency to always run my ideas past someone I trusted, first. I have worried about giving an incorrect example or sounding stupid, which would have been so humiliating.

I was the only female leader direct-report to my superior, yet I was the only direct-report without a vice president title.

Due to my risk as a Worrier, I would shut down in meetings with my superiors. I would do the same in meetings mixed with superiors and peers, paralyzed by self-doubt and a sense of inferiority. People within the organization became so familiar with my paralyzing fearful behavior that they adjusted to me. They knew I often had solutions so would prompt me, or even worse, my boss would adjourn a meeting to listen to my ideas. He would then resume the meeting later to present my ideas or my solutions while I stayed quiet. So, essentially, everyone did a "work-around" with me due to my reputation of having overwhelming fear of speaking up in the group.

I unintentionally created a self-defeating dysfunctional work environment that became the accepted "norm" by an entire division as a method of operation. With 400 people under me, I wouldn't speak up to my boss and peers at a meeting due to my Worrier risk. *(This reluctance to speak up to her boss was a combination of her Worrier traits along with her elevated risk score as a "Pleaser.")*

Over the years, as a Worrier,

- I never thought I knew enough about a new subject, no matter how much experience I had;
- I always refrained from giving my thoughts freely;
- I always second-guessed my responses when someone challenged me, even when I knew I was right.

Interestingly, as the department head of the largest department in a North America division of the industrial materials manufacturing company, my Worrier traits never arose during meetings or challenges within my direct reports and staff in my own department.

The worrying tendencies also came at bedtime for me. I was clear, concise, and decisive at my staff meetings and could field as many questions and challenges as anyone could come up with; in fact, I welcomed it. However, if there was a major decision involved, I always had a contingency plan or nagging thought that arose during the night. This caused me to run and re-run different scenarios in my head and analyze the secondary plan down to the last detail.

I finally started keeping notecards available on my night-stand to write down thoughts and ideas during the night so that I could remind myself that I had already been through this, which allowed me to relax and go back to sleep. ▪

JOANNE

A WORRIER AFTER THE FACT
Vice President, Marketing, Banking Industry

As a Worrier, I sometimes wake up at night and am not able to get a work issue from forming an endless loop in my head, preventing further sleep and any productive problem solving. These are mostly big work issues that we all have but can also be minor things that become huge frustrations.

My worrying tends to happen *after the fact* or after a decision is made. I'm actually THE change agent in my organization, the risk taker (albeit within old-school banking culture with at least some calculation behind the risk); I speak up in meetings most frequently and make decisions quickly and confidently. If only reading about the description of a Worrier and resulting indicators, I would bypass it as something I didn't relate to and ignore the lessons to be learned that can indeed hold one back from furthering her career.

My particular indicators of a Worrier are more *after* the decisions have been quickly and confidently made. And, mostly at night when I should be getting restorative, problem-solving sleep! I've tried to develop good mental health techniques to sleep better—meditation and attention to good sleeping habits. I've even considered anti-anxiety medication, but haven't wanted to resort to that just yet.

On the bright side, I tend to have a Plan B for bigger projects, and I have to say Plan B has come in very handy on numerous occasions. I also think all this late-night worrying gives me more of a 360-degree vision than most. I can and do still make decisions quickly and confidently, but I think it's been honed over many years of quickly thinking about all sides of an issue and being able to spot potential pitfalls to avoid during execution. Perhaps, too, I've learned over the years that no one likes a nay-sayer, and I've developed methods to quickly identify where problems might be and then become part of the solution.

I've rambled on too long (don't recall but probably also had elevated communication)! Then, again, I may be worrying over nothing! ∎

BRENDA

AN ASPIRING FUTURE LEADER
Consulting Firm Intern and I/O Psychology Graduate Student

I overthink my emails. It takes me too long to find a response that I am comfortable with and that I think will be perceived the *right* way. If I send an important email and don't receive a somewhat prompt response, I begin to worry that the delayed response is due to me not using the right words to express my thoughts. However, in reality, people are just busy.

As a Worrier, when I filled out job and graduate school applications, I am pretty certain that I took twice the amount of time another person would have to submit the applications. I became fixated on little details about my responses and submission instructions that most likely go unnoticed by the selection committees. I also took extra steps like researching how people have handled these applications in the past to make sure I was making the right decisions so that I didn't jeopardize my chances of being accepted. ∎

Comparing 360° Leader Feedback to Worrier, Egotist, Upstager and Rule Breaker Risk Factors

Below are quotes from narrative of the 360° review performance feedback reports of leaders who have risks in the scales highlighted in our study. This is an excerpt of a white paper presentation: "Comparing Leadership Risk Factor Results to 360° Feedback."[24] The quotes below offer clear examples of how behaviors manifest for leaders who have the respective risks. Which behaviors are tolerated more readily or viewed as being more "natural" for leaders?

CDR Risk Assessment Scales – 360° Narrative Comment

(Source: 360° Leader Scan™)

Worrier
- Is driven to achieve and works very hard; unfortunately, she is not highly productive.
- Needs to work at resolving the problems faster.
- Asks for too much info on all subjects.
- Is very indecisive—changes his mind too much.
- Not seen as change oriented or as challenging the status quo . . . has very high standards . . . needs to anticipate issues in advance.
- Consistent confidence level is an issue appears to others to be less than secure, is very capable and doesn't need to spend wasted energy being concerned about how abilities are being interpreted by others.

Rule Breaker
- I do not have access to his expense records. He is seen as a person who puts seasonal sporting events above his relationship with the staff and his job.
- He's a serial plagiarist.
- I have seen her do some rather impulsive things like sneaking into other people's confidential files.
- He's had a number of people work under him over the years and most if not all have had trouble with him before leaving or asking to be reassigned.

- I don't think anyone under him has respect for him or his work.

Egotist
- Too often, people feel as though they are his "minions" doing the dirty work while he takes the credit.
- She tends to belittle the people that interact with her by appearing to be flawless in her execution of assignments and shifting blame when mistakes are made.
- Takes credit for work done by an entire team of workers and does not acknowledge others for their extra effort.
- Admission of mistakes does not happen.
- Low level of self-awareness in terms of how his approach negatively impacts others.
- Has a hard time working with others on the team as equals. He lets it be known that he has "arrived," while they still have a long way to go.
- Has a hard time managing people "underneath" her. Often demeans and is condescending. Doesn't show the proper respect to people around her.
- Demands rather than delegates.

Upstager
- Suggest politeness and manners; needs to avoid rude interruptions.
- He consistently talks over people at company meetings.
- Takes calls during conversations. Interrupts when information is being given.
- She does not listen well, and it is hard to build any relationship with her.
- Is highly defensive and often loses a powerful message in his defensiveness.

FOUR

Cultural Bias is More Damaging Than Most Think

There is a real cultural bias that has been developed and engrained since early in the history of humankind. Normal human biases do not equate to overt or intentional, malevolent discrimination. However, leadership gender perceptions are considerably worse for women than most people think. This is where training, education, group facilitation, diversity workshops and more can help. While business people and academics alike understand this, the crux of the matter is that many leaders and professionals still buy into the biases. Many, if not most, take part by accepting or endorsing gender misperceptions without consciously realizing they are doing so or with no real grasp of the extent of the damage being done.

Alison Quirk of State Street Corp., also at the forum attended by Jack Welch, was quoted as saying, "we can all do more to help people understand their unconscious biases." [25] Ms. Quirk is right. At CDR Assessment Group, Inc., we have studied this very point:

the biases *versus* personality characteristics.

What we found is that there is a real chasm between the performance tendencies or the personality traits of women versus the related perceptions of those behaviors. It is perceptions, biases, and stereotypes that hold droves of women back while perceptions, biases, and stereotypes catapult men forward. Cracking this part of the glass ceiling is not revolutionary; however,

what is compelling is that the data are more starkly damaging from a perception standpoint than most realize.

Rubbing Salt in the Wounds: "Biases Holding Women Back"

Table 3 supports Ms. Quirk's contention that unconscious bias is holding women back far more than demonstrated performance or capability are. The table is from our presentations given at sessions for the Association of Talent Development (ATD), the Executive Women's Forum (EWF), and the Women's Business Council Southwest (WBCS), titled, "Risk Factors that Impact Women in Leadership," which shows the damaging yet different perceptions that often stem from the *same* leadership risk behavior.

TABLE 3
CDR Assessment Risk Factors and Unconscious Bias

CDR RISK ASSESSMENT SCALE DESCRIPTION	WOMEN LEADERS DEMONSTRATING THIS RISK PERCEIVED OR FREQUENTLY LABELED AS:	MEN LEADERS DEMONSTRATING THIS RISK PERCEIVED OR FREQUENTLY LABELED AS:
FALSE ADVOCATE passive-aggressive tendencies; appears outwardly supportive while covertly resisting	sneaky, spreads rumors	quiet dissenter
WORRIER unwillingness to make decisions due to fear of failure or criticism; is indecisive, over-analyzes; is self-doubting	afraid, fearful, indecisive, lacking courage	thoughtful decision maker
CYNIC is skeptical, mistrustful, pessimistic, and always looking for problems, constantly questions decisions, resists innovation	nasty, pessimistic, paranoid	investigative mind, sarcastic
RULE BREAKER ignores rules, tests the limits, does what feels good, risks company resources, does not think through consequences	inconsistent, untrustworthy	change agent, maverick

Table 3 continues on the next page.

TABLE 3 (CONTINUED)
CDR Assessment Risk Factors and Unconscious Bias

CDR RISK ASSESSMENT SCALE DESCRIPTION	WOMEN LEADERS DEMONSTRATING THIS RISK PERCEIVED OR FREQUENTLY LABELED AS:	MEN LEADERS DEMONSTRATING THIS RISK PERCEIVED OR FREQUENTLY LABELED AS:
PERFECTIONIST micro-manages, clings to details, has high need to control, has compulsive tendencies, sets unreasonably high standards	micro-manager, nitpicker	good eye for detail
EGOTIST self-centered, has sense of entitlement and superiority, takes credit for others' accomplishments, is a hard-nosed competitor	"self-absorbed bitch" (*"dragon lady"*)	overconfident
PLEASER depends on others for feedback and approval, is eager to please the boss, avoids making decisions alone, won't challenge status quo, refuses to rock the boat	ingratiating, subservient	good soldier, loyal
HYPER-MOODY unpredictable emotional swings, moodiness, volatility, potentially explosive outbursts, and vacillation of focus	too emotional or "it's that time"	intense, passionate

Table 3 continues on the next page.

TABLE 3 (CONTINUED)
CDR Assessment Risk Factors and Unconscious Bias

CDR RISK ASSESSMENT SCALE DESCRIPTION	WOMEN LEADERS DEMONSTRATING THIS RISK PERCEIVED OR FREQUENTLY LABELED AS:	MEN LEADERS DEMONSTRATING THIS RISK PERCEIVED OR FREQUENTLY LABELED AS:
DETACHED withdraws, fades away, fails to communicate, avoids confrontation, is aloof, tunes others out	non-assertive, shy	reserved, thoughtful
UPSTAGER excessively dramatic and histrionic, dominates meetings and airtime, is constantly selling a personal vision and viewpoint, demonstrates inability to go with the tide	too opinionated	sells point of view
ECCENTRIC quite unusual in thinking and behaving, perhaps whimsical, weird, out of social step or norms, peculiar in some ways	not well grounded, weird	abstract thinker

SOURCE: Nancy Parsons and Kimberly Leveridge, Ph.D., *CDR Character Assessment* (CDR Assessment Group, Inc., 1998).

Comparing CDR Assessment Results to the Pew Social Trends Survey Data

In Examples 1 through 5 below, our data further shows people are not as harsh or punitive in their judgments toward men's behaviors as they are with women's, even when the same trait or risk factor is shared. When comparing the Pew Social Trends Survey[26] results to our CDR Character and Risk Assessments, the differences are stunning.

It is clear that, as pointed out in the first part of cracking the code (Chapter 3), false perceptions and erroneous stereotypes hurt women leaders far more than they hurt men leaders. Below are five examples of what we found in comparing the Pew survey to CDR Assessment results.

Example 1

Pew survey respondents rate women as the more *emotional* sex than men by 85 percent to 5 percent.

What the CDR Assessment profile data results say:

CDR ASSESSMENT SOURCE	CDR SCALE TITLE	WOMEN LEADERS AVERAGE SCORE	MEN LEADERS AVERAGE SCORE
Character	Adjustment	50%	54%
Risk	Hyper-Moody	62%	56%

What does this mean?

- There are *no significant differences* between the "emotionality" of men and women when stress is low, based on similar Adjustment scores.
- When facing adversity, women may be slightly more emotional, according to their Hyper Moody risk factor.
- How emotionality is judged or perceived is *frequently based on gender bias.*
- For women, emotionality is often *confused* with Interpersonal Sensitivity or nurturing/caring and relationship-building capability. These are different constructs. Emotionality has to do with temperament and changing moods; high Interpersonal Sensitivity is about showing care, nurturing, kindness, and helpfulness.
- Emotionality of male leaders is often associated with anger, impatience, etc. and is considered an *accepted* behavior in most organizations. Additionally, men may be more likely to hide emotionality better than women.

Example 2

Pew survey respondents rate women as more *manipulative* than men by 52 percent to 26 percent.

What the CDR Assessment profile data results say:

CDR ASSESSMENT SOURCE	CDR SCALE TITLE	WOMEN LEADERS AVERAGED SCORE	MEN LEADERS AVERAGED SCORE
Risk	False Advocate	61%	55%
Character	Inquisitive	50%	59%
Risk	Rule Breaker	53%	64%

What does this mean?

- False Advocate is higher for women leaders so there will be more inclination for them to complain behind the scenes; can manifest as the martyr or victim syndrome.
- Men leaders may *manipulate* or "jockey for position" in bolder ways due to Rule Breaking and Inquisitive scores.
- However, the drastic difference of *52 percent to 26 percent in the Pew survey is not supported by the CDR data and* is perhaps exaggerated by biased perceptions.

Example 3

Pew survey respondents rate women as more *outgoing* than men by 47 percent to 28 percent.

What the CDR Assessment profile data results say:

CDR ASSESSMENT SOURCE	CDR SCALE TITLE	WOMEN LEADERS AVERAGED SCORE	MEN LEADERS AVERAGED SCORE
Character	Sociability	63%	57%
Risk	Upstager	60%	66%
Risk	Worrier	63%	48%

What does this mean?

- In *healthy* work environments where character strengths manifest more, women leaders are more *outgoing*.
- Under pressure and conflict, men leaders tend to be pushy and dominate airtime based on their Upstager risk.
- Under pressure, many women leaders tend to move away and not speak up, influenced by their Worrier risks.

Example 4

Pew Survey respondents rate women as more compassionate than men by 80 percent to 5 percent.

What the CDR Assessment profile data results say:

CDR ASSESSMENT SOURCE	CDR SCALE TITLE	WOMEN LEADERS AVERAGED SCORE	MEN LEADERS AVERAGED SCORE
Character	Interpersonal Sensitivity	56%	40%
Character	Sociability	63%	57%
Risk	Egotist	53%	61%

What does this mean?

- Women leaders DO tend to be more compassionate and communicate with more charm and concern based on their Interpersonal Sensitivity scores combined with their Sociability.
- Male leaders tend to be more direct due to their lower Interpersonal Sensitivity scores.
- Under stress, men may intimidate or be pushy, as indicated by their Egotist scores.
- Men leaders have a sufficient level of compassion, because they still fall within the mid-range on Interpersonal Sensitivity.

Example 5

Pew Survey respondents rate men as the more arrogant sex by 70 percent.

What the CDR Assessment profile data results say:

CDR ASSESSMENT SOURCE	CDR SCALE TITLE	WOMEN LEADERS AVERAGED SCORE	MEN LEADERS AVERAGED SCORE
Character	Adjustment	50%	54%
Risk	Egotist	52%	61%
Risk	Upstager	60%	66%

What does this mean?

- Men tend to come across as more arrogant and overly confident, particularly when facing adversity, as can be seen with their Egotist and Upstager scores.
- Arrogance is thought of as part of the common makeup of leaders (or even as acceptable). Arrogance is a trait more commonly held by men, as shown in the CDR research and the Pew survey results.

The data comparisons from the examples demonstrate that the biases are either wrong or skewed or highly exaggerated. For instance, Example #1 compares emotionality as exhibited by men and women. In the Pew survey, 80 percent of respondents rated women as the more emotional sex, compared to 5 percent for men. Yet, the personality data shows "there are no significant differences between the 'emotionality' of men and women." This means that cultural perceptions are far tougher and more harsh toward women and more forgiving of men. Men's bad behaviors are accepted or ignored. The same behaviors from women, on the other hand, can end any further upward career progress.

Why Is This Research So Compelling?

Our personality traits, both the character and the risks, are inherent, so we cannot change these in any significant way by wishing, hoping, or even training. What this means is that once we reach working-adult age, our personality traits have become our ingrained behaviors. These are set. While we can certainly enhance skills to a certain degree, we cannot change our personality traits in a major way.

For example, if someone is very extroverted, they will not become an introvert, short of a mind-altering accident or injury. The same goes for a Worrier. If one has this trait, this will also tend to present, given the stimuli and conditions that bring it about for a person. Now, training and development can help one to manage their risks more productively or even to prevent the risks from occurring in certain cases, but the tendency to worry will still appear from time to time. In Chapter 6, solutions and action plans are presented to address these issues.

Summary of Three Key Reasons
Why the Glass Ceiling Exists

#1 — Women are "Worriers"

Most illuminating and new is that women leaders are Worriers, and their own risk factors are self-defeating. This means that:

**women pull *themselves* out of the
running for promotions and upward mobility.**

Research shows that women tend to move away from conflict and adversity. By not standing their ground, they lose visibility and hurt their credibility. Many women tend to spend too much time overanalyzing and studying, versus engaging in the toughest leader discussions necessary for advancement. Women often fear speaking up when they most need to do so.

#2 — Men Move Against and Use Aggression

Men, meanwhile, have "**Egotist**," "**Upstager**," and "**Rule Breaker**" risk factors resulting in their using aggression, forcefulness, and assertive or *moving against* behaviors that claim the limelight. This makes them seem courageous and therefore seemingly more promotable or leader-like. Even though these behaviors are often dysfunctional or divisive, they are typically either viewed favorably or ignored when exhibited by men.

*#3 — Perceptions Are Often Wrong
and Much Tougher on Women*

Perceptions and cultural biases are not only present but are often wrong, and are significantly more damaging to women.

In all, these findings are good news because *the major reason why the glass ceiling hasn't been ended is because we have not clearly understood the problem.* Now that we have measured and can clearly pinpoint the crux of what is actually holding women back, we can begin implementing developmental strategies and solutions.

Chapter 5 will reveal what is different about the women who have made it past the glass ceiling to serve as CEOs or corporate executives. Chapter 6 describes solutions and outlines action plans for what we can do to end the glass ceiling for good.

FIVE

Looking at Today's Corporate Executive Women and Women CEOs

As we were completing our initial study, detailed in Chapter 2, I had a nagging curiosity. Anecdotally, I knew from assessing and coaching women executives over the years that many of them did not share the characteristics of our study group of women.

So the mystery remained: how did the few women make it past the glass ceiling to CEO and other coveted corporate executive positions? Was there a common thread or were there any particular trends or patterns?

Part 2 of Study – Profiles of Corporate Executive Women and Women CEOs

To answer this question, we began the next phase of our research. We created study groups of successful women from five different EWF International [27] Executive Peer Coaching groups from Oklahoma and Texas. We studied 22 women CEOs and 28 women corporate executives. No doubt, these women had immense determination, resolve, and talent. So many women do. But what our research has shown is there is a marked difference between the women in our original study group who were held back by the glass ceiling, and our study groups of women CEOs and other corporate executives.

How Women CEOs and Corporate Executive Women Differed from the Women in the First Study Group

First, and most important, *both the women CEO and corporate executive women groups had higher Upstager scores.* They tell, sell, become pushy, persuade, and negotiate to get their way, without backing down. As you will recall, the men leader group shared the high Upstager risk factor. Like the men, executive women and women CEOs *stay at the table and engage during conflict and adversity.* They do not retreat in fear like the women stuck beneath the glass ceiling often do.

Next, the women CEOs' scores *are nearly identical to the men leader study group's scores* when comparing their CDR Risk Factors.

The Women CEOs Are Egotists, Upstagers and Rule Breakers

So, when facing adversity, conflict and tough challenges, these women go into aggressive mode—and are willing to step up and fight and prevail. The women CEOs also scored high, similar to the male leader group, as Rule Breakers, Upstagers, and Egotists, so they will impulsively turn on a dime to achieve their goals with aggression. They may go around bureaucracies and ignore a policy or two to achieve their goals. They will also be pushy, appear courageous, and be bold in their assertions. Most of the CEOs studied were entrepreneurs.

For more information on understanding what it takes to be a successful entrepreneur, please request a copy of the article, "Assessing Your Entrepreneurial Profile" by Nancy Parsons, which was also published in Rod Robertson's book titled, *Winning at Entrepreneurship.* [28]

Illustration 3 shows the CDR Risk Assessment average scores of the four study groups. Illustration 4 only shows the four key CDR Risks compared by study group. Notice how the women CEOs and men leaders' risks align and how those who tend to get past the glass ceiling all have high Upstager scores.

ILLUSTRATION 3
CDR Risk Assessment Average Scores -
Differences in Original Study Group vs. CEOs & Corp. Executives

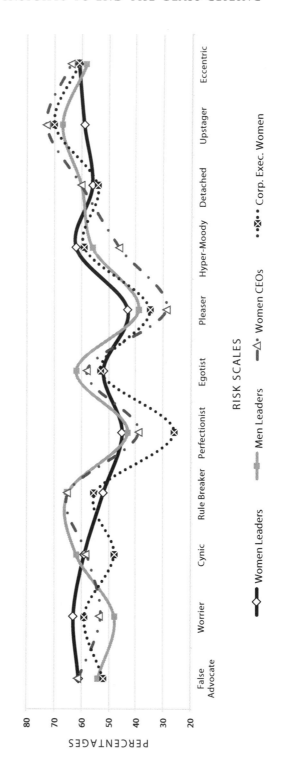

ILLUSTRATION 4
CDR Risk Assessment Average Scores - Key Group Differences

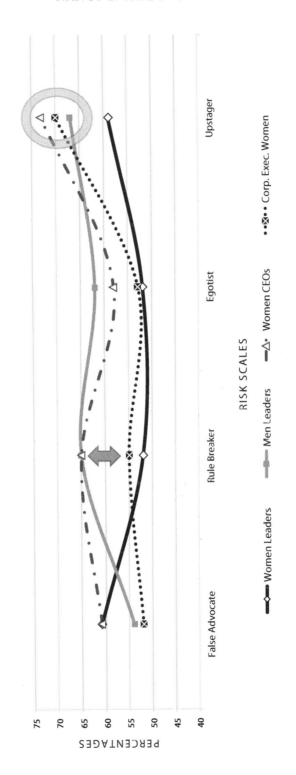

Summaries of Each Leader Group:

Men Leaders' Key Risks: Egotist, Rule Breaker, Upstager
(ORIGINAL STUDY GROUP)

Men are Moving Against, fighting for resources, fighting for airtime, and aggressively winning the day, albeit with over-the-top pushy, in-your-face, and "brave" tendencies. Men win the perception battle as they continue to push forward.

Women Leaders' Key Risk: Worrier
(ORIGINAL STUDY GROUP)

Women leaders go into Worrier or fear-of-failure and fear-of-making-a-mistake mode. They study, analyze and re-study under conflict or adversity. Their fearful, cautious, and moving-away-from-conflict approach results in women being judged as lacking courage and confidence. This is why women are disproportionately bypassed for promotions; being judged as lacking courage is a key component of the glass ceiling.

Women CEOs

Women CEOs' risk profiles are essentially the same as those of the men's study group. They have a Moving Against profile resulting in their fighting for resources, fighting for airtime, and aggressively winning the day, albeit with over-the-top pushy, in-your-face, and "brave" tendencies. Women CEOs in our study succeed as entrepreneurs because they win the perception battle as they stay in the game with stamina to fight to the end to keep their businesses surviving and thriving.

Corporate Executive Women

Corporate executive women share a mixed risk profile. They have a moderately high Worrier score. However, what helps them stay in the upward mobility race is that *they share high Upstager trends with the men and the women CEOs groups*. Notable is their low risks on False Advocate, Perfectionist, and Pleaser, suggesting that they will be direct and not work against others behind the scenes. In addition, a lower Pleaser and Perfectionist score translates into executives who do not "seek affection" when times get tough. These are positive offsets to the elevated Worrier score average.

Ineffective Coping Strategies

Interpersonal problems are often obstacles to an individual's over-all effectiveness and thus can impede an individual's ability to get along and get ahead. Self-defeating behaviors have been studied by interpersonal theorists since the 1950s. Psychoanalyst Karen Horney identified interpersonal coping strategies that can be summarized in terms of three themes: [29]

1. **Moving Toward** – going along with people in order to receive approval and affection;
2. **Moving Against** – using aggressiveness and hostility to achieve power and personal admiration; and
3. **Moving Away** – withdrawing oneself from others to achieve self-sufficiency and protection from interpersonal confrontations.

Horney's work set the stage for the study of dysfunctional dis-positions and behavior in the workplace.

In Part 1 of the CDR study, the women tended to react to adversity by Moving Away (Worriers). The men and the women CEOs tended to Move Against. From a leadership context, these ineffective coping strategies manifest as

- **Move Away** – detach, work behind the walls of your office, go silent, hold back, isolate, or just spiral into your own deep thinking and analysis (Worrier, Detached, Hyper-Moody, Cynic, and False Advocate risk factors)

- **Move Against** – become aggressive, pushy, stubborn, intim-idating, and loud, will control airtime, use a "my-way or the highway" approach, or fight hard to win the day (Upstager, Egotist, Rule Breaker, and Eccentric risk factors)

- **Move Toward** – seek to smooth things over, become overly ingratiating, help to a fault, become a "yes" person, take on too much yourself to make things better, or become unwill-ing to rock the boat or to challenge others (Perfectionist, Pleaser risk factors)

Illustration 5 shows the risk factors that are commonly associated with the Moving Away, Moving Against and Moving Toward profiles.

ILLUSTRATION 5
Risk Assesment Clusters

Risk Assessment Clusters – Traits that Commonly *"Hang Together"*

Hyper-Moody
Cynic
Worrier
Detached
False Advocate

Moving Away from People
withdrawing oneself from others to achieve self-sufficiency and protection from interpersonal confrontations

---

Egotist
Rule Breaker
Upstager
Eccentric

Moving Against People
using aggressiveness and hostility to achieve power and personal admiration

---

Perfectionist
Pleaser

Moving Toward People
going along with people in order to receive approval and affection

Below are coaching and development tips for beginning to constructively address one's ineffective coping strategies and to improve confidence, performance, communications, upward mobility, and relationships.

Understanding Those Who Commonly "Move Away"

(excerpted from Improving Your Leader Voice[30] blog series)

Leaders and professionals who tend to be more technically and financially inclined, as well as many women, usually suffer most with "moving away" tendencies. They clam up when things get tough. They hold back, rather than injecting needed commentary and views. They close their doors, seek solitude, and often dig in and work harder. They study and seek privacy versus jumping into a passionate dialogue or debate.

The performance problem that results from a team having Moving Away traits is that team members do not openly discuss the difficult issues or challenges together in order to come to the best solutions. Issues often remain avoided and unclear. Everyone stays inside his or her own head. This stress reaction of isolating oneself solidifies the separations that already likely exist. Imagine how these organizations could thrive and push forward more quickly if key leaders and teams stayed at the table to discuss the challenging issues and opportunities more openly.

Developing the "Moving Against" Leader

Many books have been written on coaching and developing leaders who have a "Moving Against" profile. These are the bullies, narcissists, and loudmouths; the pushy, overly aggressive, stubborn, argumentative, negative, weirdo, and intimidating types. This is very common in leadership because roughly 70 percent of leaders today have some level of propensity for the "Egotist" risk. Men in the study group tended to have "Moving Against" profiles.

The Moving Against profile is that of an individual who jumps to the fighting and argumentative mode when his or her buttons are pushed.

> Being raised as a Philadelphia Eagles fan and as the daughter of a union leader, this is my natural mode when the heat is on. It has taken many years of work to make reasonable headway in containing my "passion." *(I refer to it as "passion" to conveniently masque the negative aspects.)*

Leaders and professionals who Move Against are served best by hiring an executive coach who will be assertive, confident, and comfortable holding a mirror to the client's behaviors and their effect. Learning how to control the emotions, slowing down reactions, and finding tactful and appropriate ways to express dissent are all important developmental avenues for the Moving Against individual. Accountability for behaviors within organizations is most important for this type of behavior. It is not acceptable or okay to intimidate or excoriate team members or direct reports. Despite passion levels, showing respect for all is non-negotiable.

Understanding Those Who "Move Toward"

Leaders who "Move Toward" and seek affection to smooth things over often lose the respect of others. They are frequently viewed as gutless, or as those who won't stand up and fight for others, particularly when it comes to their direct reports. They may get bypassed for promotions because of being too ingratiating or agreeable. Sometimes they help too much. They are the ones who often struggle with too much work. They suffer because they cannot get the word "*no*" past their lips. They make their self-inflicted problem worse by constantly volunteering to take on extra work, despite knowing they have no time to spare. The Moving Toward risks measured by the CDR Risk Assessment are "Pleasers" and "Perfectionists". Executive assistants and administrative personnel often share both of these risk factors.

Fundamentally, Moving Toward people suffer from wanting to be "good boys" or "good girls," meaning they grew up being overly helpful and trying to be perfect. They want to please everyone. In their minds, they hope that if they only dig in and do more and do a perfect job, conflict and dissatisfaction will disappear. They especially want to satisfy and dote on authority figures.

From my 20+ years of executive coaching, the Moving Toward coping response is probably the most difficult and career-debilitating coping strategy for aspiring leaders.

However, this coping response is not hurtful or too damaging to those in certain professional roles such as executive assistants, dental assistants, nurse's aides, appointment schedulers, teacher's aides, tour guides, and similar occupations. Accountants, analysts, nurses, teachers, professors, reservations clerks, and others may have some of this coping response as well and still have solid performance, but they may need to manage these traits so that they do not go too far and interfere with their effectiveness.

Developmental suggestions for the Moving Toward profile: As a start, hire an objective, candid, and very patient executive coach who uses appropriate diagnostic assessments. Then, assertiveness training tops the list for the "Pleaser."

The "Perfectionist," which is often part of the Moving Toward package, needs to back off from their compulsive need for control, for order, and to impose their personal standards. Frequently, "Perfectionists," in the extreme, may have the deeper-rooted issue of obsessive-compulsive disorders (OCD) for which therapy may be helpful. Getting a Perfectionist leader to pull back, relax and look beyond the nagging details is a steep challenge for even the most experienced coaches.

I now encourage Perfectionists to find those executive coaches who have been successful in managing their own

Perfectionist tendencies and to learn from them. From my coaching perspective, this is a daunting risk factor to successfully coach because of the Perfectionist's inherent compulsion to get it right to the smallest degree. Having them loosen up is contrary to their comfort zone and natural approach, so it is usually a longer-term developmental commitment. That is where a patient and persistent executive coach can help.

Not to Be Overlooked: Women's Relationship-Building Skills

One other notable trend for the corporate executive women is that their Interpersonal Sensitivity scores on the CDR Character Assessment were significantly higher than all other groups, as can be seen on Illustration 6 below. [31] This means that the corporate executive women are very skilled at building and maintaining effective relationships. This helps them to navigate to higher levels and win the perception battles. This also helps them succeed and thrive within the political structures of the organization. They are also better at building effective teams, networking, serving as talent coaches and mentors, and homing in on the needs and concerns of their stakeholders, including direct reports.

Illustration 6 shows the CDR Character Assessment average scores of men and women at different leadership positions.

ILLUSTRATION 6
CDR Character Assessment Average Scores

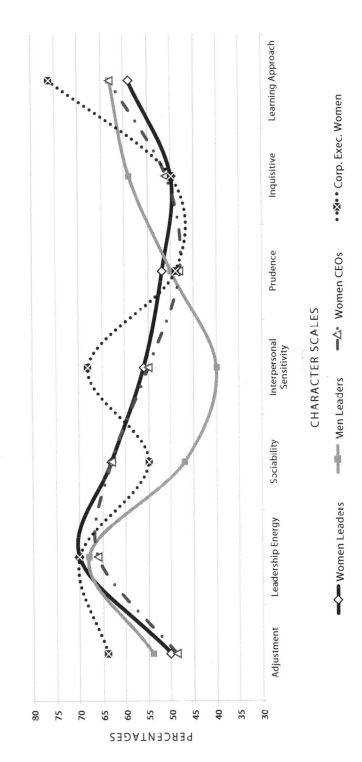

Definition, from the CDR Character Assessment report, for Interpersonal Sensitivity, the key scale difference demonstrated in Illustration 6, above:

> **INTERPERSONAL SENSITIVITY** ▪ Measures the extent to which a leader is warm, caring, and sensitive toward the needs of others, is interpersonally skilled and perceptive versus being task focused, hard-nosed, and apathetic toward the needs of others. Subscales for Interpersonal Sensitivity include cooperativeness, supportiveness, compassion, enjoyment of others, and lack of hostility.

A full listing of CDR Character scales can be found in Chapter 2.

PRE-QUIZ ANSWERS

How did you do? After reading this book and the related research, did your original responses change?

This is a key reason(s) why the glass ceiling continues to remain in place (**True or False**):

TRUE OR FALSE	KEY REASON(S) FOR THE GLASS CEILING
False	discrimination
False	the fact that women just aren't as ambitious or driven
True	promotional decision-makers favor behaviors more typically demonstrated by male leaders
False	lack of sufficient government regulations and enforcement
True	men are better at fighting for visibility and pushing their views
True	women are judged or evaluated more harshly than men
True	men are more confident in leader roles when things are tough
True	women lack courage
False	men tend to be less emotional than women
False	women are not competitive enough
False	men in leadership generally perform better than women in leadership
True	women with leadership potential often need different training or development options than men

Training Tip

This is a great quiz to open training sessions about the glass ceiling! Most people get only three or four responses correct at the pre-quiz stage.

SIX

Solutions and Action Plans

Who Owns the Problem?

Before elaborating on solutions, there must be ownership. Who owns this mess? I contend we all do. Women do. Executives do. Men do. Leadership development experts do. We all do. However, four of the most important groups that can drive the solutions forward are shown in Illustration 7:

ILLUSTRATION 7
Who Are the Glass Ceiling Solution Owners?

Each of these groups has a clear and distinct role and a responsibility to explore and implement the solutions necessary to bring down the glass ceiling for good. There will be some crossover or similar tasks involved, but the key point is that each group needs to participate.

The key to success, as with any performance initiative, is having firm commitment and accountability. For example, if the C-Suite members and board of directors fail to hold up their end of the solution, there will be no sustained success. Also, it takes senior leaders to lead the charge for a culture change. It is achievable, but it is not something you can just wish for and hope that it will turn out. The other enemy of success for executives is delegation. As mentioned previously, too many executives wash their hands of the glass ceiling when they delegate and pass the baton to a designated "diversity manager." That won't work. Diversity managers can help disseminate the message, facilitate training, and support the effort, but they should not be forced to take the lead to end the glass ceiling.

What Should Each Group Do to Bring Down the Glass Ceiling?

Illustration 8 provides an overview of what each problem owner should do to help bring down the glass ceiling.

ILLUSTRATION 8
Key Roles of Glass Ceiling Solution Owners

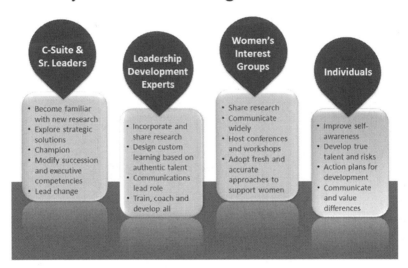

The starting point for all is to share this research. Study it. Analyze it. Debate it. Explore the implications in the organizations you serve or support. Find ways for each group to develop the solutions to this systemic problem, like those suggestions described below. Keep in mind that all groups need to begin moving in the right direction. It can't be just the women or the academics—we really need to begin a positive *movement* to break the glass ceiling.

Action Plans for the C-Suite and Senior Leaders

Executives, boards, and senior leaders need to become familiar with the research and findings shared in this book.

One of the best ways to do this is to have a facilitator at a senior level meeting, scheduling ample time to present the findings and to facilitate a dialogue with team members.

Objectives for the senior leadership team are as follows:

- **Recognize this is a real problem** that hurts the bottom line and that needs their direct support and leadership. They should explore the performance impact on their own bottom lines.
- **Realize that this is not in any way a "bash the men" or combative issue.** This is transformative for businesses because we are asking that leaders at all levels start to look more objectively and directly at what contributes to leadership success. It should be noted, the Moving Against profile frequently detracts from performance results.
- **Model the way.** Come up with solutions that will work for their business, or follow the process outlined below. Senior leaders need to serve as champions to lead the changes.

The C-Suite and Senior Leader Orientation and Discussion Process should utilize a skilled facilitator/consultant. Points to cover:

1. The glass ceiling research findings: a review of how the inherent leadership risk behavior differences under adversity often differ among men and women leaders (men Move Against and fight; women are Worriers and hold back).

2. Explore why perceptions are skewed—women are judged more harshly and negatively, often for the same behaviors exhibited by men. Consider the perceptions demonstrated in the organization.

3. A review of the consequences (including performance and financial) of allowing 1 and 2 above to hold women back. Ideally, develop a model and calculate the fiscal impact on the organization.

a. As an example, as mentioned in Chapter 1, a study of 21,980 global organizations from 91 countries conducted in 2016 by Peterson Institute for International Economics found that companies with at least 30% female leaders—in senior management positions – experienced a 15% increase in profitability. *How would an increase of about 15 percent in profitability impact the company?*

b. A study, published by MSCI Research in November 2015, of 4,000 public companies from across the globe found that "companies that had strong female leadership generated a Return on Equity of 10.1% per year versus 7.4% for those without." [32] *How would a 2.7 percent increase on return on equity impact the organization?*

c. And last, we saw how women leaders were rated higher on 360° reviews in a study by Jack Zenger and Joseph Folkman of 7,280 leaders, it was reported that "at all levels, women are rated higher in fully twelve of the sixteen leader competencies that go into outstanding leadership." [33] *How would this impact bottom line performance, employee retention and customer loyalty? Can this be measured?*

d. Look at the financial and performance indicators and run the numbers related to the positive benefits of having women in higher leadership positions.

4. Review of existing Executive Competency Models and Succession Planning Criteria. No longer should *only* those who fight with aggression under adversity be viewed as promotable or "leader-like." Discuss and consider:

a. Are the competency models, or succession planning evaluation methods, naturally screening out more women than men? Why so? Is the gap significant?

b. Equipped with the findings in this book, could a change be implemented in the current promotability ratings or developmental opportunities for women who may have high potential but who would have otherwise been ignored?

c. Do more men appear promotable because they are assertive (or even pushy) under tough or challenging situations?

    d. Do fewer women than men seem to rise to the top of succession plans or be considered for promotion?

    e. Should the Worrier trait be a valid reason *not* to consider women leadership candidates? Or is there another way to look at this or address this situation?

    f. Is the company using a scientifically valid assessment instrument to measure inherent leadership strengths and talents as well as risk factors? Should it be? What might it be missing? What does a cost/benefit analysis yield on this?

    g. Other topics, concerns, and analysis relevant to the organization and industry.

Moving forward for the C-Suite and senior leaders:

- **Be willing to dedicate** time and financial resources needed for the solution. Develop the customized authentic leadership training and individual coaching budget to help women (and men) develop their strengths while managing their differing risks. Communicate and promote this new awareness and appropriate cultural changes throughout your organization and at industry forums. Conduct employee meetings, develop short videos, and host web conferences to discuss. Begin leading the cultural shifts.

- **Gain appreciation** for the fact that leaders should be diverse in their inherent profiles (strengths and risks) and that this is a good thing. However, with the richness of diverse strengths and talents comes the need for personalized leadership development. Cookie-cutter, male-dominated leadership evaluation models and training designs are no longer viable.

- **Stop rewarding** Moving Against behaviors as the only ticket to success in the organization.

- **Review and Use the "Exploring Eight Action Plan Ideas for Change"** below in order to begin focusing on clear action plans for your team and for others to perform throughout the organization. These give you some practical steps to take.

- **Hold yourself, your team, and leaders and others throughout the organization** *accountable.* Establish and enforce leadership expectations and accountability. While it is true that all humans and leaders have some level of risk factor traits, these are not an excuse for bad behaviors.

You may want to refer to the article titled, "Are Leader Risks an Excuse for Bad Behaviors?" [34]

Action Plans for Leadership Development Experts

Leadership and talent development experts, executive coaches, diversity consultants and educators need to

- Understand that women and men all need individualized coaching with accurate assessments (as can be found in the comprehensive CDR Character Assessment, CDR Risk Assessment and CDR Drivers & Rewards Assessment). This is a critical first step to assure that you get an accurate reading on inherent strengths, risks and needs;
- Consider becoming certified in an appropriate in-depth assessment instrument that includes a risk assessment for derailment, if you are an executive coach or leadership development instructor;
- Create accurate individual learning and development plans after the assessment and review process;
- Design learning curricula that develops leaders and professionals based on a diverse competency model, not just a macho, male-oriented Moving Against model;
- Include coaching and training modules that focus on "Women as Worriers" as well as addressing other key risks of your client leaders. For example, our firm provides "Risk Factor Webinars" so that once someone is coached for their own risk factors, they can gain additional insights and training tips through these custom learning modules;
- Serve as a champion to redesign succession planning systems and executive competency models;
- Own the fact that *you* are a key catalyst and learning resource for the changes that will bring down the glass ceiling; and
- Serve as a facilitator, trainer and communicator to disseminate the research and changes throughout the organization.

Action Plans for Women's Interest Groups

Of course, women need to help women. Young and experienced alike need to provide support for one another. Therefore, I encourage women's organizations to

- Share the knowledge and research;
- Hold forums and conferences;
- Offer training and coaching;
- Offer assessments for women to begin the coaching or training process;
- Mentor and coach women on their way;
- Write, publish, and speak;
- Get creative;
- Help men to understand the inherent risk factor and perception difference; and
- Partner together to bring down the glass ceiling!

Action Plan Advice for Individuals: Women (and Men)

First and foremost—become *keenly self-aware*. Women should ask and honestly answer the tough questions about themselves:

- Do I want to lead? Or do I want to be in a professional, team member or individual contributor role?
- What are my *true or inherent strengths*?
  - Am I a natural leader—do I naturally take charge whether I'm asked to or not?
  - How comfortable am I with making decisions?
  - Do I enjoy process rather than strategy?
  - Am I good at building relationships?
  - Am I sales-oriented?
  - Do I have exceptional planning skills?
  - And the like . . .

Here's a list of seven character traits measured by the CDR Character Assessment with scoring ranges to consider:

SCALE TITLE	HIGH SCORERS TEND TO BE DESCRIBED AS:	LOW SCORERS TEND TO BE DESCRIBED AS:
Adjustment	calm, self-assured, easy-going, confident, steady under pressure and may not be sufficiently self-critical	self-critical, edgy, an intense performer, may push self and others and may not be as resilient to stress
Leadership Energy	inclined to take charge, be leader-like and decisive, be interested in upward career mobility, and be highly competitive	avoids leadership roles, prefers not to direct others and not interact with those that are concerned with upward mobility as a measure for success
Sociability	is outgoing, enjoys social interaction, is extroverted, is stimulated by talking with others	introverted tendencies: preferring less social interaction, maintaining a lower profile, keeping to oneself, being quiet and perhaps shy

Table continues on the next page.

SCALE TITLE	HIGH SCORERS TEND TO BE DESCRIBED AS:	LOW SCORERS TEND TO BE DESCRIBED AS:
Interpersonal Sensitivity	warm, caring, supportive, nurturing, sensitive toward the needs of others, is interpersonally skilled and perceptive	task focused, hard-nosed, takes an objective approach, and is apathetic toward the needs of others
Prudence	practical, conscientious, self-controlled and disciplined, steady, reliable, stable, organized and logical in a steadfast way	spontaneous, risk taking, adventurous, potentially creative, adaptable and inventive
Inquisitive	adventurous, clever, original, creative, imaginative, strategically focused and curious	practical, task and process focused, detail oriented, operationally inclined, and more down to earth
Learning Approach	typically seeks learning for the sake of personal enrichment; learns from wide range of media, and has academic interests	more interested in practical learning such as on-the-job training and hands-on or experiential learning

When thinking about your personality traits or the above CDR Character Scales, there are no good or bad scores. Ideally, what you want to do is match your traits or scores with your key job duties. If these are in alignment, you will be working toward your strengths. High and low scores can be a strength, but the preferred range varies based on the job. For example,

- A *cold-calling* salesperson would need high Sociability and low Interpersonal Sensitivity to be most successful. In this way, they would be good at initiating discussions and meeting and greeting people, yet could deal with rejection easily and would not have a need to stay attentive to the client after the sale.
- A *relationship-building* salesperson would need high Sociability with mid to mid-high Interpersonal Sensitivity. This salesperson, or account manager, would be good at taking care of customer needs and concerns for the longer haul.
- *Accountants* typically have mid to high Prudence while *software designers* have lower Prudence with high Inquisitive scores.

What Are Your Risks and Vulnerabilities?

Then, consider your risks and vulnerabilities. Everyone has some level of risks, because one's ineffective coping strategies under stress and adversity are part of normal personality.

Explore: What are my risk factors? How do I behave during conflict or with authority figures?

- Am I a Worrier? Do I fear failure or the idea of making a mistake?
- Am I a Pleaser? Am I a yes person to the boss? Do I help to a fault?
- Do I detach and go quiet when facing conflict?
- Or, do I fight and Move Against?
- Do I become a Perfectionist and have to do an extraordinary job every time?
- Am I prone to becoming too negative or critical when things go wrong?
- Is my confidence sometimes a bit overdone?
- Do I push my point of view too much or dominate air time?

Here's a list of eleven risk traits measured by the CDR Risk Assessment for you to think about:

RISK TRAIT	DEFINITION
False Advocate	has passive-aggressive tendencies; appears outwardly supportive while covertly resisting
Worrier	is unwilling to make decisions due to fear of failure or criticism
Cynic	is skeptical, mistrustful, pessimistic, always looking for problems, constantly questioning decisions, resisting innovation
Rule Breaker	ignores rules, tests the limits, does what feels good, risks company resources, does not think through consequences
Perfectionist	micro-manages, clings to details, has high need to control, has compulsive tendencies, sets unreasonably high standards
Egotist	is self-centered, has a sense of entitlement and superiority, takes credit for others' accomplishments, is a hard-nosed competitor
Pleaser	depends on others for feedback and approval, is eager to please the boss, avoids making decisions alone, won't challenge status quo, refuses to rock the boat
Hyper-Moody	has unpredictable emotional swings, moodiness, volatility, potentially explosive outbursts, and vacillation of focus
Detached	withdraws, fades away, fails to communicate, avoids confrontation, is aloof, tunes others out
Upstager	excessively dramatic and histrionic, dominates meetings and airtime, is constantly selling a personal vision and viewpoint, demonstrates inability to go with the tide
Eccentric	is quite unusual in thinking and behaving, perhaps whimsical, weird, out of social step or norms, peculiar in some ways

Developing Risks: What to Do About Your Risks?

(Adapted from: "Are Leader Risks an Excuse for Bad Behaviors?" [35])

1. Most important: Identify your specific array of risks with an appropriate assessment.
2. Next, analyze how your risks affect you. An executive or leadership coach or trained mentor is highly recommended as you work through this process. Here is an example template:

Analyzing My Risk Factors and Ways I Can Improve

The following table spans both pages.

MY RISK	WHAT CAUSED THIS RISK TO SHOW MOST RECENTLY?	HOW DID THIS RISK MANIFEST?
Upstager	Getting too energized during enjoyable discussion with colleagues	Dominated too much of the air time
Egotist	Overly eager to perform well and show my knowledge during presentation to Board	Did not sufficiently recognize the contributions of other team members
Rule Breaker	I was overly eager to close a deal with a client so I fudged the projected timeline	Although I knew that the technical department needed 90 days to implement the new software for the client, I told them it could be done in 60 days or less.
Worrier	Fear of making sure I was 100% right. I was in a staff meeting.	As a director, at a meeting with my peers and boss I knew I had the right answer, but didn't speak up. I wasn't 100% confident that someone would not find a flaw.

Analyzing My Risk Factors and Ways I Can Improve
(CONTINUED)

MY RISK	WHAT WAS THE IMPACT?	WHAT CAN I DO DIFFERENTLY?
Upstager	Came off as negative, overbearing, was a time hog	Ask more questions, self-facilitate, deploy active listening skills, control my enthusiasm
Egotist	Offended team; angered and hurt team members. Damaged team cooperativeness.	Try to relax more when I present. Build team member recognition into my presentation notes or slides so that I don't miss again! Apologize ... Rebuild ...
Rule Breaker	The technical director was furious and complained to my VP. The Tech team ended up working weekends to finish and still missed my time promise by 10 days. The client wasn't happy.	Be more genuine in communications. I can still be enthusiastic without overstating what we can do. Our technical team is top notch so I want to apologize and let them know I will honor time requirements in the future unless they approve changes in advance.
Worrier	The team made the wrong decision. Now we have to fix a costly mess which would have been avoided had I chimed in!	1) Find a mentor to help me practice speaking up in the moment. 2) Share my risks with a peer who will prompt me with questions to help bring out my thoughts. 3) Register to take an assertiveness training class.

While you cannot train or wish away your inherent risk factors, you can make big strides to improve your risk reactions under adversity. You can adopt ways to prevent, neutralize and manage these tendencies more productively. In baseball terminology, leaders can "improve their batting average" significantly when it comes to managing their risks.

What Drives You?

What are your *intrinsic motivators* and do these drivers also support your ambition to lead and in what roles? These are also known as your *deeply imbedded life interests* and they help you to find enjoyment and great satisfaction in your career and life. The following chart lists the ten CDR Drivers & Reward Assessment[36] facets we measure—which do you think you are drawn to and which do you find boring or non-interesting?

DRIVERS AND REWARDS	DESCRIPTION
Business and Finance	money, compensation or investments, economic issues
Artistic Endeavors	creative expression or interests
Companionship and Affiliation	close friendships in and outside of work
Fame and Feedback	need for recognition, respect, praise, and visibility
Humanitarian Efforts	desire for hands-on helping to directly assist the less fortunate
Amusement and Hedonism	zest for life, strong sense of humor, likes to make work fun
Power and Competition	status seeking, competitive, seeking upward mobility
Moral Platform	life revolves around unwavering values and beliefs
Scientific Reasoning	fascination with technology, scientific analysis and discovery
Safety and Security	need for long term financial, employment, and personal security

As you deepen your self-awareness, here are your next steps:

1. Ask yourself:
   a. Am I ready for this honest, deeper self-exploration process?
   b. What steps or actions do I need to take to get to my dream career goal or job?
   c. What might be slowing or stalling my success?
2. You may want to consider hiring a leadership or career coach: a skilled professional who uses validated assessments (including a risk assessment or derailment measure) to help you expedite this exploration process with accurate results. *(We can refer you . . .)*
3. Most important: *Own your career.* Your career mobility, planning, and success are your primary responsibilities.

Women who are Worriers and driven to lead: you especially must work on how to not let this risk make you seem or be judged as "not leader-like." Do not allow this risk factor to take you out of the running!

Don't wait for others to make you successful. Find where your strengths and capabilities lie, focus on what you love—and find the career that meets both of those areas for you. Remember, others can and will help you along the way; but *you own the venture.*

Eight Practical Steps to END the Glass Ceiling

Executive, leadership, and diversity teams should explore how they can best design action plans to turn the current practices and biases around in their organizations. Here are eight steps you can implement:

1. **Leadership Development and Training.** Ideally, identify *authentic leader talent* strengths, risks and motivational needs for each leader and potential leader. Develop leaders based on their inherent individual strengths, talents, gaps, risks and needs. Generic models and "group think" will not work.

2. **Design leadership development solutions that are customized to address the needs of all leaders based on their own unique profiles.** Many of the women will need development to manage and neutralize their Worrier traits more effectively. However, the key is to understand that cookie-cutter training or coaching is not suitable, because all leaders have specific, individual needs. While this research shows the trends, there are men and women leaders and high-potential staff who don't fit these trends. If a woman is a Worrier and Detached, help her develop past these vulnerabilities. If a man is an Upstager and False Advocate, help him develop past these traits to be more effective. And so on . . .

3. **Design and deliver cultural change training** throughout the organization that demonstrates how *perceptions are often wrong and are more damaging to aspiring women.* Also, share the gender research findings reported in this book. *(Please respect CDR copyrights for this research. We are glad to make a slide deck of these materials available for your use by contacting order@cdrassessmentgroup. com).* You can use our pre-post quiz and expand on this activity. This is a great topic for group brainstorming.

4. Design strategic organization-wide development, communication, promotional, succession planning and selection processes that *endorse the individual strengths and gifts of women and men. Help them manage and neutralize their specific risk factors.*

5. Clarify that the *Worrier risk trait for a woman should not be a career-ending or -blocking characteristic.* Those with

this risk factor can make improvements to be more assertive, to stay at the table, and to demonstrate improved confidence. They need to leverage their strengths to help them
neutralize and overcome this tendency.

6. Adopting objective assessment processes and leadership
coaching for high-potential leaders and staff is perhaps the
best way to improve, by identifying and developing individual talent and risks while recognizing motivational needs
and drivers.

7. Hold all leaders accountable for "bad" or inappropriate
behaviors. Acting as an intimidator or bully or hogging
airtime should not be a ticket to success any longer. Stop
giving men leaders a pass for these behaviors, and stop being harsher against women. Treating everyone with respect
should be a standard way of doing business. Men or women
who don't do this should not be promoted up the chain of
command.

8. Traditional mentoring, training, women's groups, etc. are
not making the needed inroads to bring down the glass
ceiling, although they are certainly helping women. While
these initiatives need to be continued and perhaps ramped
up, *the personnel facilitating these programs also need to
be keenly aware of the new research* results to incorporate
into their developmental processes for women.

As We Move to the *Near-Term* Future

The Glass Ceiling

- Began to disappear in late 2019 and was extinguished by late 2027 in the Western world;
- No longer stymies women's upward leadership success;
- Is not a mystery and is a problem that is largely solved based on a boost from CDR's research that identified the root cause of why it existed for so long;
- No longer costs organizations billions of dollars a year in lost opportunities;
- Stopped hindering leadership performance with effectiveness rates soaring; and
- Came down—swiftly!

Thank you. Let's get this done together!

Articles to Help Manage Leadership Risk Factors

This section includes articles to help readers understand and manage more effectively the key risks presented in this book: Worrier, Egotist, Upstager and Rule Breaker. This is a summary of the article titles and risks they cover.

ARTICLE TITLE	AUTHOR	RISK FACTOR OR DEVELOPMENTAL FOCUS
Worry Less, Lead Better	Patricia Wheeler, Ph.D.	Worrier
Can You Train "Arrogance" Out of the Organization?	Nancy Parsons	Egotist
Parallels Between "Extreme Narcissism" and the "Egotist" Leader	Nancy Parsons	Egotist
Are You a "Rule Breaker?"	Nancy Parsons	Rule Breaker
Six Leader Profiles that Reject Feedback	Nancy Parsons	Egotist, Worrier, Rule Breaker
Improving Your Leader Voice <ul><li>8 Nuances of an Effective Leader Voice</li><li>Action Plans to Improve Your Leader Voice</li></ul>	Nancy Parsons	All character traits and risk factors that interfere with leader communications and presentations

Worry Less, Lead Better

By Patricia Wheeler, Ph.D.

We've all heard the statistics. Although women make up over half the workforce, less than a quarter of them rise to middle management positions. And fewer than 10 percent ever claim a seat on their company's executive committee. These numbers haven't changed in over a decade, despite the diversity efforts of many organizations.

How do we make sense out of this? What's the problem? How much of women's lack of upward mobility is due to corporate culture that favors promotion of those who currently match the demographics of their executive chamber? And what are the parts of the equation over which talented women do wield control and influence?

As a leadership consultant and experienced executive coach, I have worked with hundreds of senior women executives over the past two decades. I know that each of the above questions have merit, and advancing more talented women to the senior level will involve addressing both. And while it's extremely important that organizations embrace and create a corporate culture that values having diverse teams, our focus here is to look through the lens of what's under a leader's own sphere of control and influence. This is where individuals can make the most immediate impact.

There's interesting and important research emerging from CDR Assessment Group. CDR President, Nancy Parsons, and her team analyzed assessment results from over 250 male and female leaders in 26 organizations (which was Part 1 of CDR's research). For those of you not familiar with CDR, they provide excellent assessments that detail one's leadership style under "normal" conditions as well as predict leaders' default styles under pressure.

So, what did they find? One important finding is that there is no significant difference between the ratings of men and women on measures of overall leadership characteristics. For example, there's no overall difference between male and female leaders in drive for results, strategic perspective, or ability to work in teams. If you've worked with as many senior women leaders as I have, this comes as no surprise. Successful leaders come in all styles.

The one factor differentiating men from women appeared in the assessment that reflects how a leader tends to behave under stress. Under pressure, women were more likely than men to respond to pressure with excessive worry. In the workplace, leaders possessing this characteristic are likely to delay making decisions due to fear of failure or criticism.

Interestingly enough, women in Parsons' research did not appear more perfectionistic than men, and as a group they did not try to please others more. But they did worry more. And what might be the effect for those of us who possess this "Worrier" derailer? Others may perceive a "Worrier" as indecisive, self-doubting, and even lacking courage, which are not the sort of behaviors that will lead to a seat on the executive committee, regardless of how smart and technically talented the leader is.

What's the best course of action for a woman who possesses the "Worrier" derailer? Here are some steps that have helped my "Worrier" clients:

1. Take a good look in the mirror. If you have this characteristic, so be it. Understand that your worry is likely to be in excess of what many situations call for. If you realize you're likely to overreact under pressure, you can plan a more adaptive response in advance. One of my clients does advance planning every time she has a meeting scheduled with her very critical boss. She asks herself what he's likely to react to negatively and mentally rehearses her messages to him. Doing so has diminished his perception that she's passive and reactive.

   Does this mean we can and should be able to eliminate worry? Of course not! Worrisome things do happen.

But knowing that you are likely to over-worry can help you anticipate situations where your "Worrier" may be triggered and plan appropriate coping strategies. Remember that this tendency need not define you and your leadership.

2. Manage your arousal. When we are under strong pressure, our biology changes. We move into a "fight or flight" mode; this causes us to create more adrenaline and cortisol. Think of these as the "unhappy neurochemicals" that help us escape actual danger (our biology hasn't really changed since we had to outrun saber-toothed tigers) but don't help us react adaptively to most workplace stresses. Recognize when you're under pressure, take a step back, and intentionally breathe more deeply and slowly. This small step actually helps our body regulate itself out of the excessive worry zone. Find ways of reminding yourself of your competence and plan in advance how you might better address recurring pressures without withdrawing into worry.

3. Embrace the positive. Scientists are finding increasing evidence that when we make the effort to acknowledge, embrace and resonate with the positive events and emotions in our life, we increase our likelihood of success. We make better decisions and we become better leaders. And we diminish the likelihood of being held captive by our derailers and default settings.

4. The even better news is that we don't need to experience intense positive emotions to reap these benefits . . . what serves us best is to create and keep the habit of acknowledging what we appreciate and what's going well in our world.

These small changes in self-awareness and behavior can help us stay out of "Worrier" and stay in our most effective leadership behaviors. This, in turn, should help many talented women advance more effectively up the leadership pipeline.

Patricia Wheeler, Ph.D. is managing partner of The Levin Group LLC (TheLevinGroup.com), a top ranked global consulting and coaching firm based in Atlanta.

Email: Patricia@TheLevinGroup.com

Copyright © 2015, Leading News, used with permission.

Can You Train "Arrogance" Out of Your Organization?

By Nancy E. Parsons

Unfortunately, you cannot train arrogance completely out of an organization. However, you can certainly make positive inroads. A significant number of leaders, roughly 70 percent, have some level of "Egotist" traits as an inherent risk factor, according to research. While this tendency shows more under adversity or conflict, this trait is part of one's personality. Under stress, this is an ineffective coping strategy that many leaders resort to in order to get their way or to deal with adversity. So, bottom line, when there is a lot of pressure and high demands in the workplace, "Egotist's" arrogant behaviors worsen.

> **The Egotist:** is self-centered, has a sense of entitlement, takes credit for others' accomplishments, is viewed as a hard-nosed competitor, has a sense of superiority, may use intimidation, and expects to be looked up to. "Egotists" often betray trust by stealing credit, creating dysfunctional work environments because of their self-obsession; fail to listen to others (because they see themselves as the smartest in the room); and they lack decision-making objectivity. Some examples of behaviors: they often put their personal agenda ahead of the needs of the team; refuse to admit mistakes or pay attention to

feedback; exhibit demeaning behaviors toward staff; and play up quite well. Last, critical feedback may not only be rejected but can cause anger, resentment, and possibly, retribution.

Keep in mind, the degree of the negativity or impact of the above behaviors will vary based on the individual's full profile and other risk factors, character strengths, job suitability, stress level, empathy, etc. For example, if someone has high "Interpersonal Sensitivity (IP)" character strength, meaning they are a caring and nurturing person, their Egotist behaviors will be diluted and not as abrasive. However, with low IP, they may behave more like be dictators, bullies or jerks, especially to people under their authority.

Once this Egotist risk trait is identified, leaders may (sometimes) manage this tendency more productively. Executive coaching and assessment is typically required for accurate, candid, hard-hitting feedback, and for guidance, review and ultimately, change. Getting an Egotist's attention is half the battle, and this is no easy quest. Once they commit to change, developing improved skills in areas such as active listening, asking better questions, tuning in to needs of staff, approaches for showing value and respect for team, etc. can be accomplished only if the commitment is strong and steadfast.

Another tactic to help neutralize the Egotist's behaviors is careful examination of what or who triggers these behaviors to manifest. Is it a peer? Is it when a mistake is made? Is it when presenting to senior leadership? Is it when someone challenges his or her idea? This should be carefully explored, ideally with a coach, so that thoughtful plans can be made to anticipate and prevent the arrogance from rearing its ugly head during future similar situations.

Keep in mind, when a leader is in a role that he or she is not well suited to perform (i.e., the square peg in a round hole), then risks, such as Egotist and one's other risks, tend to run free because this leader is under constant high stress. Other risks that are commonly found with the leader who has the Egotist risk are "Upstager" and "Rule Breaker." This compounds problematic behaviors because the Upstager will aggressively fight, argue, negotiate, and passionately push their point of view to win the day. Next, the Rule Breaker will do just that—impulsively break or violate precedence, rules, policies, values, or expectations to get their way when this trait is combined with the self-serving Egotist.

It is important to note that if Egotist behaviors are not part of the culture an organization wants to adopt or accept, steps can be taken to minimize the number of candidates selected or promoted who have this trait. One way to accomplish this is using scientifically validated pre-selection assessments to identify these traits. This, along with structured interviews and reference checking to pinpoint how these behaviors manifest for the candidate, is of great value. The assessment informs the hiring management team that the behavior is evident. Then, it is the hiring team's job to flush out the trait further to determine the impact of the behavior and candidate suitability.

Last, and most important, holding leaders accountable for their bad behaviors is essential. This is where most organizations drop the ball—especially with Egotists. While we all have various inherent risks, we also have a responsibility to manage these tendencies effectively and to treat all others with respect and dignity. Too often, organizations look the other way and tolerate these inappropriate behaviors and focus on outcomes versus how the results were achieved.

Accountability is most important because the best way to get an Egotist's attention is with clear consequences for inappropriate behaviors. This generally means walking the talk with an organization's stated core values of showing respect for all employees and stakeholders. Consequences must be real, clearly articulated, and acted upon.

This complimentary article was published at:
http://cdrassessmentgroup.com/17075-2/

and

https://www.linkedin.com/pulse/can-you-train-arrogance-out-your-organization-nancy-parsons

February 18, 2016

Parallels Between "Extreme Narcissism" and the "Egotist" Leader

By Nancy E. Parsons

With keen interest, I read Kathy Caprino's *Forbes* article, "How Extreme Narcissism Wreaks Havoc On Your Life And What To Do About It." [37] Ms. Caprino offers great insights and resources on dealing with the extreme narcissist at work and home. For her article, she interviewed expert Dr. Joseph Burgo, [38] a psychotherapist of thirty years' experience.

During the interview, Dr. Burgo identified five different types* of Extreme Narcissism, and below are four of the five that hit home in the executive coaching and assessment work we do:

The Bullying Narcissist – Builds up his or her self-image by persecuting you and making you feel like a loser.

The Seductive Narcissist – Makes you feel good about yourself, as if you're a winner, in order to secure your admiration . . . then dumps you.

The Know-It-All Narcissist – Constantly demonstrates superior knowledge in order to make others feel ignorant, uninformed, and inferior.

The Vindictive Narcissist – When challenged or wounded, will do everything possible to destroy the perceived cause of shame.

Since 1998, from a leadership context, our firm, CDR Assessment Group, Inc., has measured the inherent risk factor of "Egotist," which is a trait that reflects egocentric- or narcissistic-type behaviors for thousands of leaders around the globe in all sectors. While our instrument does not measure personality disorders (as Narcissism is categorized), the CDR Risk Assessment measures eleven leadership risk factors for those considered having "normal" personality. What this means is our database is composed of working adults (or working eligible), not clinical patients.

When used for coaching leaders and executives, the complete CDR 3-D Suite of assessments is used to reveal their full authentic talent, capability, inherent risks, and motivational needs. The Suite includes the CDR Character Assessment, CDR Risk Assessment and CDR Drivers & Rewards Assessment.

Reflecting on Dr. Burgo's four types of Extreme Narcissism above, we can see a parallel in the workplace with "Egotists" using our measures.

The Bullying "Egotist"

One who demonstrates these traits is typically in a position of power or influence. Key scores from our CDR 3-D Suite:

- **Character Assessment:** The Bullying Egotist would likely identify a person who
  - does not have empathy or concern for others (low Interpersonal Sensitivity);
  - is intense, has insecurities, and who may be emotionally volatile (low Adjustment);
  - is extroverted and outspoken (high Sociability);
  - is driven, competitive, and enjoys taking charge (high Leadership Energy).
- **Risk Assessment:** The Bullying Egotist would likely have high scores as an "Egotist," "Cynic," "Rule Breaker," "Upstager," and "Hyper-Moody"—this is what we call a "Moving Against" profile," so when dealing with conflict or a

perceived threat, they go into attack mode and can be condescending, mean, hostile and self-serving.

- **Drivers & Rewards:** High "Power and Competition," high "Fame and Feedback" are common drivers or needs that impact the Bullying Egotist because of their undaunted thirst for power, attention, and positive recognition. So, if the Bullying Egotist perceives a threat to his or her status or persona, their Moving Against risks often go into high gear.

The result is a bully or an abrasive leader who uses belittling behaviors and who treats others with a lack of respect or dignity. Below are actual excerpts of verbatim comments from Bullying Egotists' 360° feedback:

- Too often, people feel as though they are his "minions" doing the dirty work while he takes the credit.
- She tends to belittle the people that interact with her by appearing to be flawless in her execution of assignments and shifting blame when mistakes are made
- Takes credit for work done by an entire team of workers and does not acknowledge others for their extra effort.
- Low level of self-awareness in terms of how his approach negatively impacts others
- Has a hard time working with others on the team as equals. He lets it be known that he has "arrived," while they still have a long way to go.
- Has a hard time managing people "underneath" him. Often demeans and is condescending. Doesn't show the proper respect to people around him.
- Demands rather than delegates.

The Seductive "Egotist"

The Seductive-type Egotist would have higher Interpersonal Sensitivity than the Bully and would appear outwardly warm, along with high Sociability, exercising great charm and wit. They too would have a high risk factor for Egotist. (Additionally, they may also have some level of risk as a "False Advocate.") The Seductive Egotist pulls you in with their charisma, care and charm and then suddenly pounces or "dumps you" when you think the relationship is going just fine. This is also what we have experienced with leaders we have coached and refer to as the "Jekyll and Hyde" profile. Suddenly, the Seductive Egotist turns against colleagues or staff without warning and transforms into a person who is not recognizable from the warm and seemingly caring person they thought they knew.

The Know-It-All "Egotist"

By definition of this risk trait, the Egotist is a know-it-all. They are smarter, brighter, and more capable than those around them—or so they think. Here is the definition from the CDR Risk Assessment:

> **EGOTIST** ▪ This scale reveals the leader who is self-centered, has a sense of entitlement, takes credit for others' accomplishments, is viewed as a hard-nosed competitor, has a sense of superiority, and expects to be looked up to. "Egotists" betray trust by stealing credit, create dysfunctional work environments because of their self-obsession; and lack objectivity in decision making.
>
> *Examples: Putting personal agenda ahead of the needs team; refusing to admit mistakes or pay attention to feedback; and behaving like a dictator or as a pompous member of royalty.*

The Vindictive "Egotist"

Egotists of all stripes can become vindictive when crossed. By the nature of the risk factor, they reject feedback and criticism. After all, they see themselves as flawless and they are often very thin skinned. However, the most dangerous Vindictive Egotists tend to also have risks as a "False Advocate" and "Rule Breaker." The False Advocate operates behind the scenes and undermines others without their knowing until it is too late. So, revenge behind the scenes is common with the False Advocate/Egotist/Rule Breaker. Next, having the Rule Breaker risk equips the Vindictive Egotist to ignore rules, limits, or codes of ethics so that they can do whatever feels right to them for self-preservation or can get back at perceived threats. When someone outshines or goes against the Vindictive Egotist—watch out. Keep in mind, a *perceived* threat could be as simple as disagreeing in public (or at a meeting) with the Vindictive Egotist. Vengeful acts may well be brewing behind the scenes with attacks, negativity and even scheming to get back at the perceived threat or offender.

Dealing Effectively with Egotists

In determining how to deal with Egotists, a good starting place is reading Kathy Caprino's article in *Forbes* about Extreme Narcissists. Also, you may want to order Dr. Burgo's book, *The Narcissist You Know: Defending Yourself Against Extreme Narcissists in an All-About-Me World*[39] and see his blog.

With Egotists in leadership roles, the key is holding them accountable for their behaviors. It is important to identify the Egotist behaviors through comprehensive, well-constructed assessments (that measure personality-based risks) and 360° feedback. When hiring executive coaches, be sure that they have the tenacity, directness, and courage to deal directly and appropriately. Egotists will pick up on any lack of confidence or overdone kindness and this would be like blood in the water for their shark-like instincts to begin manipulating the coaching process.

One last piece of advice is that for those who are highly caring, warm, and sensitive and who may possibly have a risk factor as a "Pleaser": do *not* work for an Egotist. This can quickly become a dysfunctional relationship that is akin to the sycophant-narcissist duo. The problem with individuals with extremely high Interpersonal Sensitivity and the Pleaser risk is that they have difficulty setting boundaries, saying no, or being frank and candid. These traits make the person vulnerable to the ardent Egotist who may use and abuse them.

*Note: The fifth Extreme Narcissist type described by Dr. Burgo is the "Addicted Narcissist," and this is not a characteristic that we measure or identify in our assessment tools.

This complimentary article was published at:
http://cdrassessmentgroup.com/parallels-between-extreme-narcissism-the-egotist-leader/

and

https://www.linkedin.com/pulse/parallels-between-extreme-narcissism-egotist-leader-nancy-parsons

July 13, 2015

Are You a "Rule Breaker?"

And Five Tips to Prevent Performance Problems

By Nancy E Parsons

Do you often resist rules or procedures? Do you welcome opportunities to break the status quo and to create or build new stuff? Are you a change agent, or, sometimes, a wrecking ball? Do you have stories you could share about times you rejected authority that might surprise others? Do you enjoy being a prankster?

If so, you are probably a Rule Breaker. This is an inherent risk factor that can lead to problems on the job or can hurt your career, if gone unchecked. Obviously, this trait can also contribute to needed changes, fresh outlooks, new business ventures and creative bursts of cool new things. The question is—how do you strike the balance?

Being a Rule Breaker doesn't happen overnight. From childhood on up, our inherent risk factors develop, and by the time we are adult age these are often our natural coping responses to adversity or conflict. The Rule Breaker trait is one of the *dark sides* of personality. Interestingly, your character traits, or your bright sides, may also contribute to your lack of rule abiding (if you have low Prudence with low "Avoids Trouble" on the CDR Character Assessment measures).

I can relate this risk factor to some of my past life experiences. When I was in second grade, being raised a good Catholic girl, I was required to go to confession *every* Saturday. It was downright scary to have to go into a dark closet-like room, which was the confessional in the Church. This was a total creep out as a little girl and my heart would race like mad each time I had to go. The only light was the honeycombed yellowish screen that the priest would slide open to speak and to hear the confessor. I remember one confession at the age of seven that still stands out for me:

I said, *"Bless me Father for I have sinned, it has been one week since my last confession. Father, I lied once."* I was given five Hail Marys (prayers) to say as penance for that offense.

Here was the deal behind my confession that confirms my path in becoming a Rule Breaker. The lie I was confessing was that *I had just lied to the priest.* It had actually been *two* weeks since my last confession (due to my parents not getting us to the Church because we lived a couple miles away). I was so afraid of the priest that I lied to him. Then, trying to be a good girl, I confessed my lie.

Of course, growing up there were many other instances that I did not toe the line, exactly. For example, I remember sneaking out at night to meet boys while camping with our family. In fact, I was so good at this caper that at night I could crawl a few feet behind my parents who were sitting enjoying the campfire. A few years ago, I enjoyed buying a car with a HEMI engine so I could quickly buzz by anyone I cared to on the open highway. Of course, my job role as a business owner and entrepreneur is ideal for the Rule Breaking or non-conventional person because we have such an open canvas to create or try new "stuff."

Fortunately for me, my Rule Breaker tendencies are moderated with my need to succeed, to be perceived positively, and to be liked. (Drivers: "Power & Competition," "Fame & Feedback" and "Companionship & Affiliation.") This helps me, along with an acceptable pulse on my Prudence score—which is the conscientiousness factor.

Most Rule Breakers have some boundaries to help them not go too far. However, when coaching leaders who have high risks as Rule Breakers and who do not have strong internal moderators, one piece of advice I give them is, "Do not drink alcohol at company functions." This is because they are impulsive, and liquor zaps their limited internal regulatory sense. In one case, an organization development leader in an energy company ignored my advice. With a few drinks in him, he made the unwise decision to go skinny-dipping at the company's annual meeting offsite. Unfortunately for him, one of the newer board members saw him and really saw much more than he wanted to see. Within less than a month, that leader lost his job.

While meeting at the Pentagon with the chief learning officer and her team to discuss a rollout plan to use our assessments for their leadership development initiatives, we had an amusing exchange. She said to us,

> Well, we can't use the term Rule Breaker here that you have in the risk assessment. In the Department of Defense, everyone *must* follow the rules.

We chuckled and I said, "really, that is kind of funny, because the reason many go into the military is to break stuff."

In the end, we were good to go with using our preferred term, Rule Breaker, for all of the project work.

Here is the definition of the Rule Breaker scale from the CDR Risk Assessment Report with sample behaviors:

RULE BREAKER ▪ This scale depicts those who ignore rules, test the limits, do what feels good, jeopardize company resources, and do not think through the consequences of their behavior or decisions. In leadership roles, Rule Breakers can lose credibility and betray trust by violating rules and may be prone to fostering a dysfunctional work environment because of their impulsive and potentially destructive behavior.

Examples: Failure to comply or cutting corners with safety rules, spending more funds than expenditure authority may permit, and ignoring guidelines for appropriate Internet searches.

So, if you have Rule Breaker traits, here are some tips you can use:

1. *Test your impulsive ideas* with a trusted colleague or level-headed person before acting.
2. *Before acting, think about and write down potential consequences*, down sides or the possible negative impact on you and others.
3. *Slow down.* Breathe. Count to ten. Be more thoughtful. Take your time.
4. *Write down* the last three to five times you broke rules that caused some level of pain or concern.
   ▪ What were the triggers that set you off to act?

- Who or what prompted you to push forward with your ill-conceived impulsive behavior or reaction?
- What was the consequence or impact on you and others?

5. Last, on all three to five times from your list above, *write down a couple of ways you could have acted more thoughtfully or more appropriately for the situation.* This list provides you with insights for the next time your triggers start going off.

Recognize that your impulsiveness or prankishness can, occasionally, be fun for or add spice to what otherwise could be boring work or times. That is fine so long as you set and live within boundaries.

For example, I am impulsively writing this blog post now. I should not have sidetracked myself and spent the 45 minutes that I did on this post. This is not part of my task list or projects that I needed to attend to today. I really did not have the time to do this and it is interfering with accomplishing my work list, but this kind of thing gives me pleasure. However, I did something that hurts my planned tasks for the day, and this does put more pressure on me to finish everything else. (My team will probably roll their eyes at me—they are not Rule Breakers.) So now I can get back to work, feeling like I did something kind of fun that didn't conform to plans.

This complimentary article can be found at:
https://www.linkedin.com/pulse/you-rule-breaker-nancy-parsons

February 7, 2017

Six Leader Profiles
That Reject Feedback

By Nancy E. Parsons

When corporate executives get the boot, it is not because of their intelligence or lack of knowledge. Low self-awareness is usually the culprit. On the other hand, highly successful leaders are rooted in authenticity and are astute at building and leveraging their own true talent. There are six profile characteristics that prevent leaders from honestly looking at and owning up to their true talent. Leaders who have one or more of these profile characteristics regularly reject or dismiss feedback:

1. **Control Freaks** – these high-command and -control leaders must be responsible for all ideas and decisions; they do not welcome others' input or solutions. They reject feedback that could, in their minds, impact their grip on control or that could push them out of their comfort zone. *(CDR scales measuring this profile are: extremely high "Prudence" on the character assessment and high "Perfectionist" on the risk assessment.)*

2. **Egotists** – these leaders tend to believe themselves to be the best, smartest and brightest; play up to their superiors well; and can become incensed with negative or critical feedback. They do not want any of their imperfections or problematic behaviors to be known, as this could harm their upward

mobility and positive image, which is dear to them. They do not admit mistakes or personal shortcomings. They frequently place blame on others when things go wrong. *(CDR scales measuring this characteristic are high "No Regret" on Adjustment sub-scale on the Character and high "Egotist" on the risk assessment.)*

3. **Concealers** – these leaders are *fearful* of having others see their weaknesses or vulnerabilities, so they may push back to avoid exposure. *(CDR Risk Assessment scales identifying Concealers include any of these: "Worriers," "False Advocates," and "Cynics." They may also have low Adjustment on the character assessment.)*

4. **Defensive Do-Gooders** – these leaders tend to have very high "Interpersonal Sensitivity." They are extremely kind, nurturing, supportive, and helpful—perhaps to a fault. This individual may also lack self-criticality with high "No Regret" under Adjustment; so they tend to deflect or disregard feedback. Added to the mix of their *kind* profile, they are often also "Pleasers" and "Perfectionists" under their risk factors. This profile pushes them to seek approval, be overly helpful, and seemingly strive to be the "good boy/good girl" persona. Critical feedback *crushes* them and hurts them deeply, because they wear their feelings on their sleeves and strive so hard to be perfect and inordinately helpful to others. They depend on positive endorsement from others, and when they think others aren't delighted with them, they can go into denial, severe sadness, and become even more ingratiating, rather than dealing constructively with the feedback.

5. **Change Resisters** – these leaders resist any new or different solutions—they clearly are steadfast against change or revealing fresh approaches that may require their situation or work to change. So, rejecting feedback helps them to keep the status quo. *(Leaders with high Prudence on the CDR Character Assessment and who have "Perfectionist" and "Cynics" risk factors and high "Safety & Security" on their Drivers & Rewards Assessment often fall into this category.)*

6. **Stealth Saboteurs** – these somewhat rare profiles do not want to be found out. They work against other leaders or business objectives behind the scenes, or under the radar, to seize control with inappropriate stealth actions and behaviors. Exposure is not a viable option for them to succeed in undermining authority, leaders, or the business. They pretend to hear critical feedback because they are so charming and manipulative; meanwhile they may be seething inside with resentment, rage, and possible vengeful ambitions. Frequently, the manager or department of the Stealth Saboteur may never see the damage coming until it is too late. *(These types often have very charismatic CDR Character profiles {visible social strengths} and then have a dark mix of Rule Breaker, "False Advocate," "Egotist," and "Cynic" on their risk factors.)*

Leaders with a naturally occurring, high level of self-awareness are not as common as we might think. Most of us can self-describe at a reasonable level. However, there is not usually a deep understanding of one's composite profile and of the connectedness and impact of specific behavioral predispositions. Through nearly two decades of assessment work and executive coaching, we have found that the best way for executives and leaders to quickly become self-aware of their strengths, inherent risks and motivation with unrivaled individual specificity, is through a debrief with their CDR 3-D Suite, measuring leadership Character, Risks for Derailment, and Drivers & Reward needs.

We have coached thousands of executives around the globe and have had only three or four executives in all that time who, after going through the self-awareness assessment and coaching, have dug in their heels and said something like:

"Well, that is who I am . . . and my people will just need to deal with it."

In the end, failure to accept and address the impact of one's risks or ineffective behaviors is a losing proposition for a leader. Every leader has true talent, strengths, gifts and needs. Every leader also has *built-in baggage* when it comes to performance with their personal assortment of risk factors. These are one's ineffective coping behaviors that undermine effectiveness.

Gone unchecked or allowed to run amok, risk factors have thrown the careers of even the most prominent executives off track. Of the handful of executives we worked with who outright rejected the importance of paying attention to and doing something productive with their assessment results, *all* were eventually fired or forced out and replaced. Their decision to expect others to *just deal with them as they were* did not pay off.

> One such CEO, Allen, who led a large retail organization, craved constant personal updates and busy work by executives over the weekends and around the clock. While the information he demanded was not necessary or particularly helpful to the business, he said he just wasn't comfortable without the 24/7 updates. As his coach, I let Allen know the negative toll his behavior was taking on his team based on feedback from his executive team. He refused to deal with his obsessive need for detail and control. Despite the candid feedback and stress level he imposed, he said he just *couldn't* let go. Well, funny how things work out—the Board let him go. We have other stories of C-Suite executives of *Fortune* 500 organizations who rejected similar feedback who have been ousted as well.

Authenticity alone is not the ticket to successes. Being open and responsive to feedback, and then focusing on continued development, is the key. Self-aware leaders who welcome in-depth, frank feedback are clear about their strengths, even the nuances of their greatest capabilities, and are able to leverage these. Exceptionally self-aware leaders are open about their inherent risks, and work each day to keep those from interfering with their relationships and leadership effectiveness. They look for ways to continue to develop themselves and to grow. They share their personal development growth experiences, stories, triumphs, and setbacks with their people, and regularly request feedback. They model development and inspire their staff members to develop in turn. Exceptional leaders are authentic leaders who are willing to own up to who they are and to continue to grow their true talent. In turn, they are better equipped to support the growth and performance of others with compassion, objectivity, and courage.

When leaders complete their initial coaching debrief session, providing them a deep appreciation and clarity around their true talent, we commonly hear: "I wish I had done this twenty years ago." One commented, "I feel like you unzipped my skin and looked inside of my soul." Even the most cynical types going in to the coaching debrief, come out of the coaching session with a renewed and refreshed heightening of their self-awareness.

The reality is that many leaders work relentlessly and the majority do not take time out to refresh, renew, and take a personal inventory of their true capability, vulnerabilities, needs, and career and life goals. Experiencing in-depth, accurate and unvarnished coaching feedback with tools in the genre of the CDR 3-D Suite for profound self-awareness, is like a spa for the mind, work spirit, and personal ambition.

This complimentary article can be found at:
http://cdrassessmentgroup.com/six-leader-profiles-that-reject-feedback/

and

https://www.linkedin.com/pulse/six-leader-profiles-reject-feedback-nancy-parsons

December 16, 2015

Improving Your Leader Voice

Part 1 – Eight Nuances of an
Effective Leader Voice

By Nancy E. Parsons

Having a clear and inspiring leader voice is a tremendous asset for a leader. Unfortunately, this is a struggle for many, particularly those who have strong technical and financial backgrounds. Leaders whose comfort zones and key strengths reside within the sciences and financial aspects of the business are often moderate-level communicators at best.

Being on the less-communicative side helps them to be great listeners, pay attention to all insights, and be thoughtful, deliberate communicators. So frequently when they speak, it is with profound value and impact. The downside is that these noteworthy contributions are typically not injected often enough. This leaves others to fill in the cracks, make leaps, and assume. This in turn can create uncertainty and, potentially, strategic and tactical missteps and disconnects for the team and organization.

To improve communications, particularly if you are a technical or financial authority at heart, it is important to measure your starting point. What are your natural talents and gaps when it comes to communications? Your review should be sliced down to a nuanced level so that you can clearly identify, with laser focus, where you may need to develop. Being specific rather than too broad in scope is important to making and sustaining the success needed.

What, precisely, is causing your possible deficiencies or lack-luster communications approach? Is there an area or two you can tweak to make marked improvements, or will you need to take a deeper developmental dive? Is it worth it to you? What are the alternatives approaches, if any, for you to consider? The point is, if you are a raging introvert who would rather have a root canal than give a presentation, perhaps developing this gap is not a productive or worth-while endeavor for you.

Here are eight leader voice nuances (characteristics and motivational facets) to consider that impact your success:

1. **Comfort Level** – In a leadership capacity, how is your presentation confidence?
   a. Do all presentations or opportunities to chime in at meetings cause you anxiety or give you sweaty palms?
   b. Do you tend to over-prepare for planned presentations?
   c. Do you dread spontaneous presentation opportunities?
   d. Are you more comfortable with some groups rather than others (your peers vs. the board of directors?)
   e. Do you welcome any opportunity to present to any group?

2. **All Eyes on You**
   a. Do you enjoy the limelight and being the center of attention?
   b. Are you one who tends to take control at meetings?
   c. Would you prefer to let someone else take center stage while you remain in the background?

3. **Natural Charm and Wit**
   a. When you present or speak, do you enjoy being entertaining?
   b. Do you relish telling stories and jokes, and comfortably find ways to put others at ease?
   c. When you are at social gatherings, are you known for being a go-to person who leads entertaining or stimulating conversations?
   d. Do you tend to be more factual with data and information when you present—just getting to the point without embellishing with stories, banter, etc.?

NANCY E. PARSONS

4. **Candor**
   a. Are you comfortable being frank with stakeholders?
   b. Do you have difficulty being direct and clear?
   c. Are you able to give candid feedback or views to others without delaying or sugar-coating the message?

5. **Energy**
   a. Does engaging with others at meetings energize you?
   b. Does face time or meetings with others wear you out after a fairly short time?
   c. When you are alone does your energy pick up more than when you are with others?
   d. How long can you tolerate being in meetings with people each day and still feel refreshed?

6. **Openness**
   a. Are you an open book when communicating?
   b. Do you prefer to be close to the vest and only communicate to others certain information on a need-to-know basis?
   c. Would you consider yourself private and not caring to share your deeper thoughts or feelings with colleagues or stakeholders?
   d. Is it somewhat hard for others to get to know you, and do you keep people at a "safe" distance, especially early on?
   e. Do you sometimes tend to give too much information? Have you ever been told you give too many details and need to keep it higher level?
   f. Are you brutally honest to the point of sometimes making others uncomfortable or defensive?

7. **Executive Presence and Inspirational Approach**
   a. Are you confident in your approach, or do you continually second guess or criticize yourself inside your head?
   b. Does your body language promote leader confidence?
   c. Do you project the expected image of an executive in your industry?
   d. Are you known for inspiring others, and are you viewed as a role model?
   e. Are you the realist who focuses on why things won't work? Do you tend to be the one looking out for things that are likely to go wrong?

123

   f. Do you pride yourself in being a one-of-a-kind or as a free spirit who marches to your own tune?

8. **Joy of Visibility and Attention – Intrinsic Motivator and Driver**
   a. Do you enjoy and welcome opportunities to have public praise or recognition, or do you find public praise humiliating or distasteful?
   b. Is speaking in front of others something you enjoy, or is public speaking something you abhor or find unpleasant?
   c. Is the notion of giving effective presentations and speaking up more often something you really would find rewarding, or, if truth be known, you would rather not do? Deep down, do you prefer to let someone else do more of the presenting?

Your responses to each of the questions above will help you to delineate and clarify your gaps, areas of greatest discomfort, and specific opportunities to target. It may be helpful for you to rate yourself in the above traits so that you can pinpoint and prioritize where you most need to sharpen your capabilities in order to make the furthest inroads in improving your leader voice. Once you clarify your targeted growth points, it is time to begin to brainstorm and formulate tangible and measurable development plans for improvement.

Another idea that can be useful is that once you think you are close to having your game plan for development finalized, hold a stakeholder review session with your team. You can share a high level of your self-assessment with them (your strengths and gaps), share your tentative ideas for development, and ask them for input. Do they agree that your action ideas are worthwhile and are the best way to achieve success? Perhaps they have other suggestions to support your development. Stakeholder feedback can be of great value in many areas of building your leadership capacity and success.

Blogger's Recommendation:

To maximize and accelerate success, I recommend you

1. utilize the services of a qualified executive coach or communications coach;
2. take a validated assessment (like the CDR 3-D Suite) to accurately measure the nuanced character traits, motivational drivers, and risks that can impede your effectiveness; and
3. develop a written action plan with clear goals, actions, resources needed, time frames and how success will be measured. Then, execute your plan!

This complimentary article can be found at:
http://cdrassessmentgroup.com/8-nuances-of-an-effective-leader-voice/

and

https://www.linkedin.com/pulse/8-nuances-effective-leader-voice-nancy-parsons

May 18, 2016

Improving Your Leader Voice

Part 2 – Action Plan Ideas to
Improve Your Leader Voice

By Nancy E Parsons

All Eyes on You and *Natural Charm and Wit*

Let's say you are quite comfortable being in the limelight and presenting, but you tend to be rather dry, direct and a *deliverer-of-the-facts-only* kind of presenter. Many with engineering and financial backgrounds share these traits. First, it is important to own these distinctions. Since you are an adult whose personality traits cannot be changed in a dramatic way, you cannot be trained to be *naturally* witty, charming, and at great ease in telling stories. You can, however, make clear improvements with your strengths and make some inroads in your inherent gaps. Below are some developmental suggestions for the dry, informational presenter:

1. Keep your presentations *short!* Do not drag or drone on with excessive facts! Try to
    a. make your presentation as concise as possible; use bulleted bites of information only; use pictures—they are better than words on slides; and, if you feel compelled to provide details, offer these in handout materials and do not include in presentation slides;
    b. take frequent breaks;
    c. break up the presentation segments by adding discussion or problem-solving sessions to engage and energize attendees;
    d. co-present or join with, when possible, someone who is naturally more compelling and at ease. It can add an entertaining mix to have two opposing styles in action. Do not co-present with someone who is similarly an "informational" presenter. (Many years ago I, along with several energy industry executives, attended a several-days session titled "Introduction to Coal Mining" taught by *two* information-presenter-style engineers. It was excruciating, nearly painful, to sit through.)

2. Make sure meetings are well facilitated so that the pace moves effectively with participation and energy levels kept high. Practice your presentations—video and watch yourself. Audio record. You can do this in the car with your iPhone. Redo. Get feedback from others. What can be improved? Test new approaches. Practice more to increase your confidence.

3. Find a mentor or coach to give you feedback and candid suggestions.

4. With your key stakeholders, be open about your communications approach as an information provider. Ask for feedback and ideas. Share your newly established goals and ask for their support and suggestions.

5. Consider changing the openings to your presentations. Do not start with the facts and introductions as you normally would. Start with an outcome that went badly or a personal experience that might intrigue attendees. Share the impact and lessons learned. Then, move into the related subject matter. This naturally gains more interest of the meeting participants than beginning with a standard "Hello, my

name is Nancy and I am going to talk to you about widgets, colored widgets, fat and skinny widgets . . . *snooze, snooze* . . ."

Related story:

My oldest daughter, Katie, is past the halfway point of a prestigious MBA program. She's a chemical engineer and has worked in food and beverage manufacturing management for nearly ten years; she formerly was a production manager for a large global brewer. As part of an MBA class assignment, she had to give a five-minute talk on a subject she was knowledgeable about. Beer was an obvious subject choice for her. She talked to me about the upcoming presentation. She naturally had lots of facts about types of beers, beer processing, ingredients, and other less-than-compelling beer-making details.

I asked her why she didn't start with interesting insights about her personal experience with beer (not counting her college days . . .). So, we began to talk and recall her history. She had been the youngest Brewing Ambassador for the company at the age 24 while in Williamsburg, VA. While she brewed beer by day, in the evenings and weekends as a Beer Ambassador she was to meet and greet local restaurant guests and buy them complimentary beer. Not a bad deal. She also met her husband brewing beer. Back then, he managed bottling and packaging operations for the company. She included these types of personal stories into her presentation, and she was a true sensation. She received outstanding reviews by combining personal stories and technical know-how in a way that surprised and piqued the interest of everyone.

Book Recommendation and Presentation Training: The above suggestion about changing your opening, along with many more highly effective approaches, can found in the book: *Own the Room* by David Booth and Deborah Shames and Peter Desberg. [40] They also provide exceptional workshops and personal coaching to improve your presentation skills. Their firm is *Eloqui.* [41] Their workshops involve a great deal of practice, new techniques and lots of feedback.

You can improve your leader voice if you are committed to doing so. Assess your strengths and weaknesses, get feedback, formulate action plans, and include lots of practice to gain confidence and improve your skills. Join organizations like *Toastmasters* [42] to get practice presenting to a live audience. Like it or not, being an effective presenter is pivotal to leadership success, so perhaps it is time for you to get to work.

This complimentary article can be found at:

https://www.linkedin.com/pulse/action-plan-ideas-improve-your-leader-voice-nancy-parsons http://cdrassessmentgroup.com/action-plan-ideas-to-improve-your-leader-voice/

June 28, 2016

APPENDIX II

Research Methodology

The research in this book essentially involved three steps:

- Compared inherent personality risk assessment results of mid-level men and women leader study groups to determine if there were any notable gender differences.
- Analyzed personality character and risk assessment results compared to Pew Cultural Survey Results of the perceptions men and women leaders.
- Compared the personality data (character and risks) of the first study groups to data of the second study group of corporate executive women and CEO/entrepreneurial women groups.

The Study Participants

In the first study that is shared in Chapter 3, we reviewed the CDR Risk Assessment results of mid-level leaders: 137 women and 122 men from 35 companies. In our second study, reported in Chapter 4, we analyzed the personality assessment results (character and risk assessments) of 30 corporate executive women and 21 women CEOs/entrepreneurs who were members of six different EWF International groups. Leaders in both of our studies were from more than 80 companies.

CDR Personality Assessments Used in the Research

"Personality assessment is useful for describing an individual's characteristics that may not be directly observed. Behaviors are visible to people, but the reasons behind them and the motivations for them are not observable. Psychological assessment results provide a vocabulary for describing propensities and a view of the "whys" behind the behaviors. This information in turn allows for more effective employee selection, succession planning, team building, and professional development."[43] In our studies related to the glass ceiling, we used personality measure results from the CDR Risk Assessment and CDR Character Assessment.

Companies and Sectors of Participants in Study Groups

The leaders in our studies were from more than eighty companies; below are samples of sectors the leaders represent:

- Banking/Finance
- Energy
- Pharmaceutical
- Medical Device
- Healthcare
- Entertainment
- Retail
- Manufacturing
- Real Estate
- Logistics
- Food Industries
- Education/Academia
- Federal Government
- Department of Defense
- Insurance
- Transportation
- Chemical
- Publishing
- Marketing/Advertising
- Utilities
- Communications/Media
- Service/Consulting

Women's Organizations and Participation

EWF International provided us with participant access to obtain the data for our second study. EWF International was formed in 1998 and has created and facilitated peer advisory forum groups for women business owners and executives. [44] We worked with EWF's "CEO" and "Corporate Executive Women's" peer executive groups. We worked with a total of six groups that were based in Tulsa, Oklahoma City and Dallas, Texas.

We also facilitated workshops for these women's forums during which we reviewed our research results and provided group leadership training. In addition, we held workshops to debrief the Character, Risks, and in some cases, Drivers Assessment results with all of the participating women executives. Many of these executive women also opted to go through one-on-one coaching with their CDR 3-D Suite results.

Pew Cultural Survey

The Pew Cultural Survey Report that summarized key trends over time in the movement of women into leadership positions in politics, business, the labor force and the professions was used in this book. In Chapter 5, we introduced the cultural bias of men versus women and then compared the Pew survey results to CDR Personality Character and Risk Assessment results.

CDR Assessment Validity Process

When developing a personality assessment, the first question to answer is what to measure. Items are then written to reflect the behaviors associated with the dimension(s) being measured. For example, extroversion is defined as: interest in or behavior directed toward others. Thus, items to measure extroversion might be written to indicate the degree to which a person enjoys (or does not enjoy) social settings, crowded events, and making presentations. Sample items focusing on extroversion might be "in a group, I enjoy attracting attention to myself" or "I don't care for large, noisy crowds."

Once a pool of test items are written—pool size is determined by the number of dimensions being assessed and the number of items deemed necessary to tap into each dimension—the items are pilot tested to determine the degree to which they correlate with each other, they differentiate people (some endorse, some do not), and they are reliable. Reliability is determined by test-retest—subjects answer the question the same way on multiple administrations—and by internal consistency—items which are designed to measure extroversion tend to correlate, or hang-together.

The next step is to determine the validity of the measure, which is a bit more complicated to explain. First, there is what's known as the test-test validation process, which correlates scores on our instruments with other instruments. These test-to-test correlations are conducted with instruments that are hypothesized to have similar or related constructs and with instruments that are hypothesized to be unrelated. For example, the process of validating a tool like the CDR Character Assessment includes having subjects take that instrument along with others such as the ASVAB, PSI Basic Skills Test, Myers-Briggs Type Indicator, Self-Directed Search (SDS), Interpersonal Adjective Scales, Big-Five Factor Markers assessment, and the Minnesota Multiphasic Personality Inventory-2 (MMPI-2). These analyses result in correlations used to confirm hypothesized relationships.

The next level of validation included correlations between test scores and relevant non-test indicators, such as actual performance ratings. This step was taken to validate (confirm or not) whether the instrument accurately measures the predicted behavior and the impact on performance. For example, those who have high scores on the CDR Character Assessment Adjustment scale and a high CDR Risk Assessment "Egotist" score will generally have higher self-ratings on 360° performance reviews. This translates to people having higher opinions about their own performance in comparison with the perceptions of others. Thus, the correlations will be higher between these scale scores and the resulting behavior ratings. The validation process is not simple and it is important to perform statistical analyses using a variety of non-test indicators and performance results. In addition to performance reviews, other examples of non-test indicators may include: sales results, customer retention, customer complaints, accidents, turnover, errors, etc.[45]

When developed in 1998, for CDR's Character Assessment and the CDR Risk Assessment, we used an existing database with well-established norms and data that had over 300,000 and 100,000 cases respectively.

About the Author

Nancy Parsons is one of today's foremost experts in combining the science of assessments with the art of developing people. Since 1998 she has served as president of CDR Assessment Group, Inc., which she co-founded with Kimberly Leveridge, Ph.D. Together, they created the breakthrough CDR 3-Dimensional Assessment Suite®, a coaching and leadership measurement tool that has been translated into five languages.

Parsons provides executive coaching for C-Suite executives and leaders, facilitates strategic executive-team development, instructs "Authentic Leadership" workshops, and teaches CDR Executive Coaches' Certification Workshops for internal and external consultants. She has published more than 30 articles and is currently completing her second book, Unvarnished Leadership, which is about identifying and developing one's inherent leadership capabilities. Parsons has presented at international, national, and regional professional conferences including ATD and Women in Leadership.

In addition to her professional activities, Parsons leads the philanthropic initiative "Vets Coaching Vets," and is a member of both the Alexcel Group and CoachSource global executive coaching organizations. She resides in Sugar Land, Texas with her husband and three very spoiled dogs. To learn more about Nancy Parsons and the CDR Assessment Group, Inc., visit www.cdrassessmentgroup.com.

About CDR Assessment Group, Inc.

www.cdrassessmentgroup.com
Twitter: @CDR_Assessment & cdrinfo@cdrassessmentgroup.com

We are a globally recognized assessment and leadership and talent development firm leading the way with revolutionary products, executive coaching and consulting services, research, and training solutions.

We are committed to providing cutting-edge leadership and talent development products and services for global clients, designed with the foremost psychological insights and applied business know-how.

Our Assessments

CDR 3-Dimensional Assessment Suite®

- CDR Character Assessment
- CDR Risk Assessment
- CDR Drivers & Rewards Assessment
- Reports available: full interpretive developmental, staffing/selection, team, succession planning, and more, available in five languages.

360° Leader Scan™

- Multi-rater leadership performance and development instrument containing approximately 80 items, 10 core competency areas, and statistical and narrative input

Executive Team Performance Forecast™ and Strategic Team Analysis

Surveys, Research, and Custom Products

Our Services for Women in Leadership

1. Presentations on this book topic: Keynote, Conference; Executive/Leadership Workshops (2-4 hours)
2. Accelerated Leadership Coaching using CDR 3-D Suite
3. Women's Leadership Workshop *(see description at the end of this section)*
4. Coaches' Certification Workshops and Train the Trainer for Women's Leadership Workshops

Key Services

CDR-U – Talent Development

- Executive Coaching (We have a global team of CDR Certified Executive Coaches available for client projects.)
- Authentic Leadership Programs
- Women in Leadership Workshops
- Strategic Team Development
- Executive Coaches' Certification and Advanced Training
- Selection Screening Process Training
- Risk Factors Webinars
- CDR-U.com and Online Learning

CDR-TM – Talent Management

- Leadership Capability Analysis
- Selection Screening

- Succession Planning
- Executive Team Performance Forecasts
- Interventions, Root Cause Analysis Projects
- Cultural and Incentive Studies
- Research Projects

Women's Leadership Workshop

Experts from CDR Assessment Group, Inc. and affiliated executive coaches offer this powerful and unmatched leadership development experience, exclusively for women.

This is no ordinary or generic event. Women, if you are ready for a life-changing experience to zero in on your leadership strengths, emotional intelligence, personal needs and risk factors, then this is a must-attend for you.

This development process will:

- Enhance your confidence and leadership presence
- Explore and rekindle your strengths and motivations
- Bolster your authentic leadership acumen
- Identify your "secret sauce" for exceptional leadership
- Enhance your influence in male-dominated cultures
- Develop your approach to break through the glass ceiling
- Build your confidence to ask the tough questions
- Prepare you to deal with conflict more effectively
- Improve the balance between your professional and personal life
- Develop and sustain strategies for ongoing learning and growth

Women's Leadership Workshop includes:

1. Two-day custom workshop lead by two expert instructors
2. CDR 3-D Suite: Leadership Character, Risks, and Drivers & Rewards Assessments
3. One-to-one executive coaching (2.5 hours) prior to workshop and one post-workshop session
4. Personal branding, mission statement and developmental action plan.

Notes

1   "Women CEOs of the S&P 500," *Catalyst*, Apr. 25, 2017,
    http://www.catalyst.org/knowledge/women-ceos-sp-500.

2. "The Pregnancy Discrimination Act of 1978." *U.S. Equal Employment Opportunity Commission*,
    https://www.eeoc.gov/laws/statutes/pregnancy.cfm.

3. Ann Morrison, et al., *Breaking the Glass Ceiling: Can Women Reach the Top of America's Largest Corporations?* (Addison-Wesley Pub. Co., 1987), 13.

4. "Women CEOs of the S&P 500," *Catalyst*, Apr. 25, 2017.

5. Matt Egan, "Still Missing: Female Business Leaders," *CNNMoney*, Mar. 24, 2015, http://money.cnn.com/2015/03/24/investing/female-ceo-pipeline-leadership/.

6. "The 2016 State of Women-Owned Businesses Report," *American Express OPEN*, Apr. 2016, http://www.womenable.com/content/userfiles/2016_State_of_Women-Owned_Businesses_Executive_Report.pdf.

7. David Beede and Robert Rubinovitz, "Utilization of Women-Owned Businesses in Federal Prime Contracting," *U.S. Department of Commerce*, Dec. 31, 2015,
    https://www.sba.gov/sites/default/files/wosb_study_report.pdf.

8. "Men and Women: No Big Difference," *American Psychological Association*, Oct. 20, 2005,
    www.apa.org/research/action/difference.aspx.

9. Jack Zenger and Joseph Folkman, "Are Women Better Leaders than Men?," *Harvard Business Review*, Mar. 15, 2012, https://hbr.org/2012/03/a-study-in-leadership-women-do.

10. Chris Bart and Gregory McQueen, "Why Women Make Better Directors." *International Journal of Business Governance and Ethics* 8, no. 1 (2013): 95. http://www.boarddiversity.ca/sites/default/files/IJBGE8-Paper5-Why-Women-Make-Better-Directors.pdf.

11. Linda-Eling Lee, et al. "Women on Boards." *MSCI Inc.*, November 2015, https://www.msci.com/documents/10199/04b6f646-d638-4878-9c61-4eb91748a82b.

12. Marcus Noland and Tyler Moran. "Study: Firms with More Women in the C-Suite Are More Profitable." *Harvard Business Review*, Feb. 8, 2016, https://hbr.org/2016/02/study-firms-with-more-women-in-the-c-suite-are-more-profitable.

13. John Bussey, "Women, Welch Clash at Forum," *The Wall Street Journal*, May 4, 2012, https://www.wsj.com/articles/SB10001424052702303877604577382321364803912?mg=id-wsj.

14. "Women and Leadership," *Pew Research Center*, Jan. 14, 2015, http://www.pewsocialtrends.org/2015/01/14/women-and-leadership/.

15. Matt Symonds, "10 Traits of Women Business Leaders: They're Not What You Think," *Forbes*, Aug. 8, 2012, https://www.forbes.com/sites/mattsymonds/2012/08/08/10-traits-of-women-business-leaders-its-not-what-you-think/#4e4cbdb515c2.

16. "The Glass Ceiling: How Women Are Blocked from Getting to the Top," *Feminist Majority Foundation*, http://www.feminist.org/research/business/ewb_glass.html.

17. "Harvard IOP Spring 2016 Poll," *Harvard IOP,* Apr. 25, 2016, http://iop.harvard.edu/youth-poll/harvard-iop-spring-2016-poll.

18. Catherine Stupp, "The Brief: 2016: The Year Women Banged Their Heads Against the Glass Ceiling," *Euractiv*, Nov. 10, 2016, http://www.euractiv.com/section/all/news/the-brief-2016-the-year-women-banged-their-heads-against-the-glass-ceiling/.

19. Nancy Parsons, "Comparing Leadership Risk Factor Results to 360° Feedback," *CDR Assessment Group, Inc.*, Oct. 2015, http://cdrassessmentgroup.com/wp-content/uploads/2015/10/CDR-Leader-Risks-and-360-Comparisons.pdf.

20. "Men and Women: No Big Difference," *American Psychological Association*, Oct. 20, 2005, http://www.apa.org/research/action/difference.aspx.

21. Nancy Parsons and Kimberly Leveridge, *CDR Risk Assessment* (CDR Assessment Group, Inc., 1998).

22. Ibid.

23. Sheryl Sandberg, *Lean In: Women, Work and the Will to Lead* (New York: Knopf Doubleday Publishing Group, 2013), 3.

24. Parsons, "Comparing Risk Factor to 360° Feedback."

25. Natasha Gural, "How State Street Is Bypassing Recruiters To Attain Its Top Tier Hiring Targets," *eFinancialCareers*, Jul. 9, 2013, http://news.efinancialcareers.com/us-en/145706/how-state-street-is -bypassing-recruiters-to-attain-its-top-tier-hiring-targets/.

26. "Men or Women: Who's the Better Leader?," *Pew Research Center*, Aug. 25, 2008, http://www.pewsocialtrends.org/2008/08/25/men-or -women-whos-the-better-leader/.

27. http://ewfinternational.com/.

28. Rod Robertson, *Winning Entrepreneurship Insiders' Building Business* (Issaquah: Made for Success Publishing, 2014). https://www.amazon.com/Winning-Entrepreneurship-Insiders -Robertson-2014-10-07/dp/B01FJ1AHQQ/ref=sr_1_2?ie=UTF8&qid =1501882827&sr=8-2&keywords=Winning+Entrepreneurship +Insiders+Building+Business.

29. Karen Horney, *Our Inner Conflicts: A Constructive Theory of Neurosis* (New York: W. W. Norton & Company, 1992), 14–16.

30. Nancy Parsons, "How Conflict and Adversity Can Detract from Your Leader Voice." *CDR Assessment Group, Inc.*, Jan. 26, 2016, http://cdrassessmentgroup.com/conflict-adversity-can-detract -leader-voice/.

31. Nancy Parsons and Kimberly Leveridge, *CDR Character Assessment* (CDR Assessment Group, Inc., 1998).

32. Linda-Eling Lee, et al. "Women on Boards." MSCI Inc., November 2015.

33. Jack Zenger and Joseph Folkman, "Are Women Better Leaders than Men?," *Harvard Business Review*, Mar. 15, 2012.

34. Nancy Parsons, "Are Leader Risks an Excuse for Bad Behaviors?," May 2017, www.cdrassessmentgroup.com/publications/.

35. Ibid.

36. Nancy Parsons and Kimberly Leveridge, *CDR Drivers & Rewards Assessment* (CDR Assessment Group, Inc., 1999).

37. Kathy Caprino, "How Extreme Narcissism Wreaks Havoc On Your Life And What To Do About It," *Forbes*, Jul. 6, 2015. https://www.forbes.com/sites/kathycaprino/2015/07/06 /how-extreme-narcissism-wreaks-havoc-on-your-life-and -what-to-do-about-it/#7dc980f715d2.

38. http://www.josephburgo.com/.

39. Joseph Burgo, *The Narcissist You Know* (New York: Touchstone; Reprint Edition, 2015), https://www.amazon.com/Narcissist-You -Know-Narcissists-All-About-Me/dp/1476785686/.

40. David Booth, Deborah Shames, Peter Desberg, *Own the Room: Business Presentations that Persuade, Engage, and Get Results*, (McGraw Hill Education; 1 edition, 2009). https://www.amazon.com/Own-Room-Business-Presentations -Persuade/dp/0071628592/ref=sr_1_1?ie=UTF8&qid =1501900833&sr=8-1&keywords=Own+the+Room%3A +Business+Presentations+that+Persuade%2C+Engage%2C +and+Get+Results%2C.

41. http://eloqui.biz/.

42. https://www.toastmasters.org/.

43. Kimberly Leveridge, "Summary of Test Development" (CDR Assessment Group, Inc., 2004), p 3.

44. http://ewfinternational.com/about-ewf-international/.

45. Kimberly Leveridge, "Summary of Test Development" (CDR Assessment Group, Inc., 2004).

45857706R00092

Made in the USA
Lexington, KY
21 July 2019